Essential Hymn Collection

kevin
mayhew

Acknowledgements

The publishers wish to express their gratitude to the copyright holders who have granted permission to include their material in this book.

Every effort has been made to trace the copyright holders of all the songs in this collection and we hope that no copyright has been infringed. Apology is made and pardon sought if the contrary be the case, and a correction will be made in any reprint of this book.

Important Copyright Information

We would like to remind users of this hymnal that the reproduction of any song texts or music without the permission of the copyright holder is illegal. Details of all copyright holders are clearly indicated under each song.

Many of the song *texts* may be covered either by a Christian Copyright Licensing (CCL) licence or a Calamus licence. If you possess a CCL or Calamus licence, it is essential that you check your instruction manual to ensure that the song you wish to use is covered.

If you are *not* a member of CCL or Calamus, or the song you wish to reproduce is not covered by your licence, you must contact the copyright holder direct for their permission.

Christian Copyright Licensing (Europe) Ltd., have also now introduced a *Music Reproduction Licence*. Again, if you hold such a licence it is essential that you check your instruction manual to ensure that the song you wish to reproduce is covered. The reproduction of any music not covered by your licence is both illegal and immoral.

If you are interested in joining CCL or Calamus they can be contacted at the following addresses:

Christian Copyright Licensing (Europe) Ltd. P.O. Box 1339, Eastbourne, East Sussex. BN 21 1AD.
Tel: 01323 417711, Fax: 01323 417722

Calamus, 30 North Terrace, Mildenhall, Suffolk, IP28 7AB.
Tel: 01638 716579, Fax: 01638 510390.

First published in Great Britain in 2002 by
KEVIN MAYHEW LIMITED
Buxhall, Stowmarket
Suffolk IP14 3BW

Compilation © Kevin Mayhew Ltd 2002

The right of Kevin Mayhew to be identified as the compiler and editor of this work has been asserted by them in accordance with the Copyright, Designs and Patents Act 1988.

The following editions are available.

Words edition	Catalogue No.1413211	
	ISBN No. 1 84003 958 2	ISMN No. M 57024 115 6
Large Print edition	Catalogue No.1413215	
	ISBN No. 1 84003 959 0	ISMN No. M 57024 116 3
Full Music edition	Catalogue No. 1413214	
	ISBN No. 1 84003 957 4	ISMN No. M 57024 114 9

Cover design by Angela Selfe
Cover photograph by Nicky Dillon, Lambourn, Berkshire
Printed & Bound By The Bath Press, Bath

Foreword

In *Essential Hymn Collection* it has been our aim to gather together hymns and songs which are universally loved by Christians, thus providing a collection that can be used comfortably by all who raise their voice in worship of God.

It is something Jesus would have been familiar with in the temple, and he certainly sang at the Last Supper, for, according to Matthew: 'After psalms had been sung they left for the Mount of Olives.'

And the apostle Paul, writing to the Ephesians, was another enthusiast: 'Sing hymns and psalms to the Lord with praise in your hearts.'

What a wonderful faith we share!

THE PUBLISHER

1

Dave Bilbrough
© 1977 Thankyou Music

Abba, Father, let me be
yours and yours alone.
May my will for ever be
more and more your own.
Never let my heart grow cold,
never let me go.
Abba, Father, let me be
yours and yours alone.

2

Henry Francis Lyte (1793-1847)

1. Abide with me,
   fast falls the eventide;
   the darkness deepens;
   Lord, with me abide:
   when other helpers fail,
   and comforts flee,
   help of the helpless,
   O abide with me.

2. Swift to its close
   ebbs out life's little day;
   earth's joys grow dim,
   its glories pass away;
   change and decay
   in all around I see;
   O thou who changest not,
   abide with me.

3. I need thy presence
   ev'ry passing hour;
   what but thy grace can foil
   the tempter's pow'r?
   Who like thyself my guide
   and stay can be?
   Through cloud and sunshine,
   Lord, abide with me.

4. I fear no foe
   with thee at hand to bless;
   ills have no weight,
   and tears no bitterness.
   Where is death's sting?
   Where, grave, thy victory?
   I triumph still,
   if thou abide with me.

5. Hold thou thy cross
   before my closing eyes;
   shine through the gloom,
   and point me to the skies;
   heav'n's morning breaks,
   and earth's vain shadows flee;
   in life, in death, O Lord,
   abide with me.

3

St. Germanus (c. 634-c. 734) trans.
John Mason Neale (1818-1866) alt.

1. A great and mighty wonder,
   a full and holy cure!
   The Virgin bears the infant
   with virgin-honour pure:

   Repeat the hymn again!
   'To God on high be glory,
   and peace on earth shall reign.'

2. The Word becomes incarnate,
   and yet remains on high;
   and cherubim sing anthems
   to shepherds from the sky:

3. While thus they sing your monarch,
   those bright angelic bands,
   rejoice, ye vales and mountains,
   ye oceans, clap your hands:

4. Since all he comes to ransom
   by all be he adored,
   the infant born in Bethl'em,
   the Saviour and the Lord:

4 William Henry Draper (1855-1933) alt.
© J. Curwen & Sons Ltd.

1. All creatures of our God and King,
   lift up your voice and with us sing
   alleluia, alleluia!
   Thou burning sun with golden beam,
   thou silver moon with softer gleam:

   O praise him, O praise him,
   alleluia, alleluia, alleluia!

2. Thou rushing wind that art so strong,
   ye clouds that sail in heav'n along,
   O praise him, alleluia!
   Thou rising morn, in praise rejoice,
   ye lights of evening, find a voice:

3. Thou flowing water, pure and clear,
   make music for thy Lord to hear,
   alleluia, alleluia!
   Thou fire so masterful and bright,
   that givest us both warmth and light:

4. Dear mother earth, who day by day
   unfoldest blessings on our way,
   O praise him, alleluia!
   The flow'rs and fruits that in thee grow,
   let them his glory also show.

5. All you with mercy in your heart,
   forgiving others, take your part,
   O sing ye, alleluia!
   Ye who long pain and sorrow bear,
   praise God and on him cast your care:

6. And thou, most kind and gentle death,
   waiting to hush our latest breath,
   O praise him, alleluia!
   Thou leadest home the child of God,
   and Christ our Lord the way hath trod:

7. Let all things their Creator bless,
   and worship him in humbleness,
   O praise him, alleluia!
   Praise, praise the Father, praise the Son,
   and praise the Spirit, Three in One.

5 Donald Fishel (b. 1950)
© 1973 Word of God Music Administered by CopyCare

Alleluia, alleluia,
give thanks to the risen Lord,
alleluia, alleluia, give praise to his name.

1. Jesus is Lord of all the earth.
   He is the King of creation.

2. Spread the good news o'er all the earth.
   Jesus has died and is risen.

3. We have been crucified with Christ.
   Now we shall live for ever.

4. God has proclaimed the just reward:
   'Life for us all, alleluia!'

5. Come, let us praise the living God,
   joyfully sing to our Saviour.

6 Christopher Wordsworth (1807-1885)

1. Alleluia, alleluia,
   hearts to heav'n and voices raise;
   sing to God a hymn of gladness,
   sing to God a hymn of praise:
   he who on the cross a victim
   for the world's salvation bled,
   Jesus Christ, the King of Glory,
   now is risen from the dead.

2. Christ is risen, Christ the first-fruits
   of the holy harvest field,
   which will all its full abundance
   at his second coming yield;
   then the golden ears of harvest
   will their heads before him wave,
   ripened by his glorious sunshine,
   from the furrows of the grave.

3. Christ is risen, we are risen;
   shed upon us heav'nly grace,
   rain, and dew, and gleams of glory
   from the brightness of thy face;
   that we, with our hearts in heaven,
   here on earth may fruitful be,
   and by angel-hands be gathered,
   and be ever, Lord, with thee.

4. Alleluia, alleluia,
   glory be to God on high;
   alleluia to the Saviour,
   who has gained the victory;
   alleluia to the Spirit,
   fount of love and sanctity;
   alleluia, alleluia,
   to the Triune Majesty.

7 William Chatterton Dix (1837-1898) alt. the editors
© *This version 1999 Kevin Mayhew Ltd.*

1. Alleluia, sing to Jesus,
   his the sceptre, his the throne;
   alleluia, his the triumph,
   his the victory alone:
   hark, the songs of peaceful Sion
   thunder like a mighty flood:
   Jesus, out of ev'ry nation,
   hath redeemed us by his blood.

2. Alleluia, not as orphans
   are we left in sorrow now;
   alleluia, he is near us,
   faith believes, nor questions how;
   though the cloud from sight received him
   when the forty days were o'er,
   shall our hearts forget his promise,
   'I am with you evermore'?

3. Alleluia, bread of angels,
   here on earth our food, our stay;
   alleluia, here the sinful
   come to you from day to day.
   Intercessor, friend of sinners,
   earth's redeemer, plead for me,
   where the songs of all the sinless
   sweep across the crystal sea.

4. Alleluia, King eternal,
   he the Lord of lords we own;
   alleluia, born of Mary,
   earth his footstool, heav'n his throne;
   he within the veil has entered
   robed in flesh, our great High Priest;
   he on earth both priest and victim
   in the Eucharistic Feast.

8 William John Sparrow-Simpson (1859-1952) alt.
© *Novello & Co. Ltd.*

1. All for Jesus! All for Jesus!
   This our song shall ever be;
   for we have no hope nor Saviour
   if we have not hope in thee.

2. All for Jesus! thou wilt give us
   strength to serve thee hour by hour;
   none can move us from thy presence
   while we trust thy love and pow'r.

3. All for Jesus! at thine altar
   thou dost give us sweet content;
   there, dear Saviour, we receive thee
   in thy holy sacrament.

4. All for Jesus! thou hast loved us,
   all for Jesus! thou hast died,
   all for Jesus! thou art with us,
   all for Jesus, glorified!

5. All for Jesus! All for Jesus!
   This the Church's song shall be,
   till at last the flock is gathered
   one in love, and one in thee.

9 St Theodulph of Orleans (d. 821)
trans. John Mason Neale

All glory, laud and honour,
to thee, Redeemer King,
to whom the lips of children
made sweet hosannas ring.

Continued overleaf

1. Thou art the King of Israel,
thou David's royal Son,
who in the Lord's name comest,
the King and blessed one.

All glory, laud and honour,
to thee, Redeemer King,
to whom the lips of children
made sweet hosannas ring.

2. The company of angels
are praising thee on high,
and mortals, joined with all things
created, make reply.

3. The people of the Hebrews
with palms before thee went:
our praise and prayer and anthems
before thee we present.

4. To thee before thy passion
they sang their hymns of praise:
to thee now high exalted
our melody we raise.

5. Thou didst accept their praises,
accept the prayers we bring,
who in all good delightest,
thou good and gracious king.

10 Edward Perronet (1726-1792)
adapted by Michael Forster (b. 1946)
© This version 1999 Kevin Mayhew Ltd.

1. All hail the pow'r of Jesus' name,
let angels prostrate fall;
bring forth the royal diadem

and crown him, crown him, crown him,
crown him Lord of all.

2. Crown him, all martyrs of your God,
who from his altar call;
praise him whose way of pain you trod,
and crown him . . .

3. O prophets faithful to his word,
in matters great and small,
who made his voice of justice heard,
now crown him . . .

4. All sinners, now redeemed by grace,
who heard your Saviour's call,
now robed in light before his face,
O crown him . . .

5. Let every tribe and every race
who heard the freedom call,
in liberation, see Christ's face,
and crown him . . .

6. Let every people, every tongue
to him their heart enthral:
lift high the universal song
and crown him . . .

11 Tricia Richards
© 1987 Thankyou Music

1. All heav'n declares
the glory of the risen Lord.
Who can compare
with the beauty of the Lord?
For ever he will be
the Lamb upon the throne.
I gladly bow the knee
and worship him alone.

2. I will proclaim
the glory of the risen Lord.
Who once was slain
to reconcile us all to God.
For ever you will be
the Lamb upon the throne.
I gladly bow the knee
and worship you alone.

12 Graham Kendrick (b. 1950), based on Philippians 3:8-12
© 1993 Make Way Music

1. All I once held dear, built my life upon,
all this world reveres, and wars to own,
all I once thought gain I have
counted loss;
spent and worthless now, compared
to this.

Knowing you, Jesus, knowing you,
there is no greater thing.
You're my all, you're the best,
you're my joy, my righteousness,
and I love you, Lord.

2. Now my heart's desire is to know
   you more,
   to be found in you and known as yours.
   To possess by faith what I could not earn,
   all-surpassing gift of righteousness.

3. Oh, to know the pow'r of your risen life,
   and to know you in your sufferings.
   To become like you in your death,
   my Lord,
   so with you to live and never die.

13 Robert Bridges (1844-1930), based on 'Meine Hoffnung stehet feste' by Joachim Neander (1650-1680)

1. All my hope on God is founded;
   he doth still my trust renew.
   Me through change and chance
   he guideth,
   only good and only true.
   God unknown, he alone
   calls my heart to be his own.

2. Human pride and earthly glory,
   sword and crown betray his trust;
   what with care and toil he buildeth,
   tow'r and temple, fall to dust.
   But God's pow'r, hour by hour,
   is my temple and my tow'r.

3. God's great goodness aye endureth,
   deep his wisdom, passing thought:
   splendour, light and life attend him,
   beauty springeth out of naught.
   Evermore, from his store,
   new-born worlds rise and adore.

4. Still from earth to God eternal
   sacrifice of praise be done,
   high above all praises praising
   for the gift of Christ his Son.
   Christ doth call one and all:
   ye who follow shall not fall.

14 Roy Turner
© 1984 Thankyou Music

1. All over the world the Spirit is moving,
   all over the world,
   as the prophets said it would be.
   All over the world there's a mighty
   revelation
   of the glory of the Lord,
   as the waters cover the sea.

2. All over this land the Spirit is
   moving . . .

3. All over the Church the Spirit is
   moving . . .

4. All over us all the Spirit is
   moving . . .

5. Deep down in my heart the Spirit
   is moving . . .

15 William Kethe (d. 1594)

1. All people that on earth do dwell,
   sing to the Lord with cheerful voice;
   him serve with fear, his praise forth tell,
   come ye before him and rejoice.

2. The Lord, ye know, is God indeed,
   without our aid he did us make;
   we are his folk, he doth us feed
   and for his sheep he doth us take.

3. O enter then his gates with praise,
   approach with joy his courts unto;
   praise, laud and bless his name always,
   for it is seemly so to do.

Continued overleaf

4. For why? the Lord our God is good:
   his mercy is for ever sure;
   his truth at all times firmly stood,
   and shall from age to age endure.

5. To Father, Son and Holy Ghost,
   the God whom heav'n and earth adore,
   from us and from the angel-host
   be praise and glory evermore.

16 Cecil Frances Alexander (1818-1895)

All things bright and beautiful,
all creatures great and small,
all things wise and wonderful,
the Lord God made them all.

1. Each little flow'r that opens,
   each little bird that sings,
   he made their glowing colours,
   he made their tiny wings.

2. The purple-headed mountain,
   the river running by,
   the sunset and the morning
   that brightens up the sky.

3. The cold wind in the winter,
   the pleasant summer sun,
   the ripe fruits in the garden,
   he made them every one.

4. The tall trees in the greenwood,
   the meadows for our play,
   the rushes by the water,
   to gather ev'ry day.

5. He gave us eyes to see them,
   and lips that we might tell
   how great is God Almighty,
   who has made all things well.

17 18th century-Latin
trans. Edward Caswall (1814-1878) alt. the editors
© 1999 This version Kevin Mayhew Ltd.

1. All you who seek a comfort sure
   in trouble and distress,
   whatever sorrow vex the mind,
   or guilt the soul oppress.

2. Jesus, who gave himself for you
   upon the cross to die,
   opens to you his sacred heart;
   O, to that heart draw nigh.

3. You hear how kindly he invites;
   you hear his words so blest:
   'All you that labour, come to me,
   and I will give you rest.'

4. What meeker than the Saviour's heart?
   As on the cross he lay,
   it did his murderers forgive,
   and for their pardon pray.

5. Jesus, the joy of saints on high,
   the hope of sinners here,
   attracted by those loving words
   to you I lift my prayer.

6. Wash then my wounds in that dear blood
   which forth from you does flow;
   by grace a better hope inspire,
   and risen life bestow.

18 Christopher Ellis (b. 1949)
vs 1-4 John Newton (1725-1807) alt.
v 5 John Rees (1828-1900)

1. Amazing grace! How sweet the sound
   that saved a wretch like me.
   I once was lost, but now I'm found;
   was blind, but now I see.

2. 'Twas grace that taught my heart to fear,
   and grace my fears relieved.
   How precious did that grace appear
   the hour I first believed.

3. Through many dangers, toils and snares
   I have already come.
   'Tis grace that brought me safe thus far,
   and grace will lead me home.

4. The Lord has promised good to me,
   his word my hope secures;
   he will my shield and portion be
   as long as life endures.

5. When we've been there a thousand years,
   bright shining as the sun,
   we've no less days to sing God's praise
   than when we first begun.

19 Charles Wesley (1707-1788)

1. And can it be that I should gain
   an int'rest in the Saviour's blood?
   Died he for me, who caused his pain?
   For me, who him to death pursued?
   Amazing love! How can it be
   that thou, my God, shouldst die
      for me?

   Amazing love! How can it be
   that thou, my God, shouldst die for me?

2. 'Tis myst'ry all! th'Immortal dies:
   who can explore his strange design?
   In vain the first-born seraph tries
   to sound the depths of love divine!
   'Tis mercy all! Let earth adore,
   let angel minds inquire no more.

3. He left his Father's throne above
   so free, so infinite his grace;
   emptied himself of all but love,
   and bled for Adam's helpless race;
   'tis mercy all, immense and free;
   for, O my God, it found out me.

4. Long my imprisoned spirit lay
   fast bound in sin and nature's night;
   thine eye diffused a quick'ning ray,
   I woke, the dungeon flamed with light;
   my chains fell off, my heart was free;
   I rose, went forth, and followed thee.

5. No condemnation now I dread;
   Jesus, and all in him, is mine!
   Alive in him, my living Head,
   and clothed in righteousness divine,
   bold I approach the eternal throne,
   and claim the crown, through Christ
      my own.

20 William Blake (1757-1827)

1. And did those feet in ancient time
   walk upon England's mountains green?
   And was the holy Lamb of God
   on England's pleasant pastures seen?
   And did the countenance divine
   shine forth upon our clouded hills?
   And was Jerusalem builded here
   among those dark satanic mills?

2. Bring me my bow of burning gold!
   Bring me my arrows of desire!
   Bring me my spear! O clouds unfold!
   Bring me my chariot of fire!
   I will not cease from mental fight,
   nor shall my sword sleep in my hand,
   till we have built Jerusalem
   in England's green and pleasant land.

21 William Bright (1824-1901)

1. And now, O Father, mindful of the love
   that bought us, once for all, on Calv'ry's
      tree,
   and having with us him that pleads above,
   we here present, we here spread forth to
      thee
   that only off'ring perfect in thine eyes,
   the one true, pure, immortal sacrifice.

2. Look, Father, look on his anointed face,
   and only look on us as found in him;
   look not on our misusings of thy grace,
   our prayer so languid, and our faith so
      dim:
   for lo, between our sins and their reward
   we set the Passion of thy Son our Lord.

Continued overleaf

3. And then for those, our dearest and our
     best,
   by this prevailing presence we appeal:
   O fold them closer to thy mercy's breast,
   O do thine utmost for their souls' true
     weal;
   from tainting mischief keep them pure
     and clear,
   and crown thy gifts with strength to
     persevere.

4. And so we come: O draw us to thy feet,
   most patient Saviour, who canst love us
     still;
   and by this food, so aweful and so sweet,
   deliver us from ev'ry touch of ill:
   in thine own service make us glad and
     free,
   and grant us never more to part with
     thee.

22

v 1 unknown, based on John 13:34-35
vs 2-4 Aniceto Nazareth, based on John 15 and 1 Cor. 13
© 1984, 1999 Kevin Mayhew Ltd.

A new commandment I give unto you:
that you love one another as I have loved you,
that you love one another as I have loved you.

1. By this shall all know
   that you are my disciples
   if you have love one for another. *(Repeat)*

2. You are my friends
   if you do what I command you.
   Without my help you can do nothing.
   (Repeat)

3. I am the true vine,
   my Father is the gard'ner.
   Abide in me: I will be with you. *(Repeat)*

4. True love is patient,
   not arrogant nor boastful;
   love bears all things, love is eternal.
   (Repeat)

23

James Montgomery (1771-1854)

1. Angels from the realms of glory,
   wing your flight o'er all the earth;
   ye who sang creation's story
   now proclaim Messiah's birth:

   Come and worship
   Christ, the new-born King:
   come and worship,
   worship Christ, the new-born King.

2. Shepherds, in the field abiding,
   watching o'er your flocks by night,
   God with us is now residing,
   yonder shines the infant Light:

3. Sages, leave your contemplations;
   brighter visions beam afar:
   seek the great Desire of Nations;
   ye have seen his natal star:

4. Saints before the altar bending,
   watching long in hope and fear,
   suddenly the Lord, descending,
   in his temple shall appear:

5. Though an infant now we view him,
   he shall fill his Father's throne,
   gather all the nations to him;
   ev'ry knee shall then bow down:

24

Francis Pott (1832-1909) alt.

1. Angel-voices ever singing
   round thy throne of light,
   angel-harps for ever ringing,
   rest not day nor night;
   thousands only live to bless thee,
   and confess thee Lord of might.

2. Thou who art beyond the farthest
   mortal eye can see,
   can it be that thou regardest
   our poor hymnody?
   Yes, we know that thou art near us
   and wilt hear us constantly.

3. Yea, we know that thou rejoicest
   o'er each work of thine;
   thou didst ears and hands and voices
   for thy praise design;
   craftsman's art and music's measure
   for thy pleasure all combine.

4. In thy house, great God, we offer
   of thine own to thee;
   and for thine acceptance proffer
   all unworthily,
   hearts and minds and hands and voices
   in our choicest psalmody.

5. Honour, glory, might and merit,
   thine shall ever be,
   Father, Son and Holy Spirit,
   blessèd Trinity.
   Of the best that thou hast given
   earth and heaven render thee.

25 Martin Nystrom, based on Psalm 42:1-2
*© 1983 Restoration Music Ltd.
Administered by Sovereign Music UK*

1. As the deer pants for the water,
   so my soul longs after you.
   You alone are my heart's desire
   and I long to worship you.

   *You alone are my strength, my shield,
   to you alone may my spirit yield.
   You alone are my heart's desire
   and I long to worship you.*

2. I want you more than gold or silver,
   only you can satisfy.
   You alone are the real joy-giver
   and the apple of my eye.

3. You're my friend and you are my brother,
   even though you are a king.
   I love you more than any other,
   so much more than anything.

26 John Daniels
*1979 Word's Spirit of Praise Music
Administered by CopyCare*

As we are gathered, Jesus is here;
one with each other, Jesus is here;
joined by the Spirit, washed in the blood,
part of the body, the church of God.
As we are gathered, Jesus is here;
one with each other, Jesus is here.

27 William Chatterton Dix (1837-1898)

1. As with gladness men of old
   did the guiding star behold,
   as with joy they hailed its light,
   leading onward, beaming bright;
   so, most gracious Lord, may we
   evermore be led to thee.

2. As with joyful steps they sped,
   to that lowly manger-bed,
   there to bend the knee before
   him whom heav'n and earth adore,
   so may we with willing feet
   ever seek thy mercy-seat.

3. As their precious gifts they laid,
   at thy manger roughly made,
   so may we with holy joy,
   pure, and free from sin's alloy,
   all our costliest treasures bring,
   Christ, to thee our heav'nly King.

4. Holy Jesu, ev'ry day
   keep us in the narrow way;
   and, when earthly things are past,
   bring our ransomed souls at last
   where they need no star to guide,
   where no clouds thy glory hide.

Continued overleaf

5. In the heav'nly country bright
need they no created light,
thou its light, its joy, its crown,
thou its sun which goes not down;
there for ever may we sing
alleluias to our King.

28 'Ad regias Agni dapes'
trans. Robert Campbell (1814-1868)

1. At the Lamb's high feast we sing
praise to our victorious King,
who hath washed us in the tide
flowing from his piercèd side;
praise we him, whose love divine
gives his sacred blood for wine,
gives his body for the feast,
Christ the victim, Christ the priest.

2. Where the paschal blood is poured,
death's dark angel sheathes his sword;
faithful hosts triumphant go
through the wave that drowns the foe.
Praise we Christ, whose blood was shed,
paschal victim, paschal bread;
with sincerity and love
eat we manna from above.

3. Mighty victim from above,
conqu'ring by the pow'r of love;
thou hast triumphed in the fight,
thou hast brought us life and light.
Now no more can death appal,
now no more the grave enthral:
thou hast opened paradise,
and in thee thy saints shall rise.

4. Easter triumph, Easter joy,
nothing now can this destroy;
from sin's pow'r do thou set free
souls new-born, O Lord, in thee.
Hymns of glory and of praise,
risen Lord, to thee we raise;
holy Father, praise to thee,
with the Spirit, ever be.

29 Caroline Maria Noel (1817-1877)

1. At the name of Jesus
ev'ry knee shall bow,
ev'ry tongue confess him
King of glory now;
'tis the Father's pleasure
we should call him Lord,
who, from the beginning,
was the mighty Word.

2. At his voice creation
sprang at once to sight,
all the angels' faces,
all the hosts of light,
thrones and dominations,
stars upon their way,
all the heav'nly orders
in their great array.

3. Humbled for a season,
to receive a name
from the lips of sinners
unto whom he came,
faithfully he bore it,
spotless to the last,
brought it back victorious
when from death he passed.

4. Bore it up triumphant
with its human light,
through all ranks of creatures
to the central height,
to the throne of Godhead,
to the Father's breast,
filled it with the glory
of that perfect rest.

5. In your hearts enthrone him;
there let him subdue
all that is not holy,
all that is not true;
crown him as your captain
in temptation's hour;
let his will enfold you
in its light and pow'r.

6. Truly, this Lord Jesus
   shall return again,
   with his Father's glory,
   with his angel train;
   for all wreaths of empire
   meet upon his brow,
   and our hearts confess him
   King of glory now.

7. Direct, control, suggest, this day,
   all I design or do or say;
   that all my pow'rs, with all their might,
   in thy sole glory may unite.

   This Doxology is sung after either part

8. Praise God, from whom all blessings
     flow,
   praise him, all creatures here below,
   praise him above, angelic host,
   praise Father, Son and Holy Ghost.

30 Thomas Ken (1637-1711) alt.

1. Awake, my soul, and with the sun
   thy daily stage of duty run;
   shake off dull sloth, and joyful rise
   to pay thy morning sacrifice.

2. Redeem thy mis-spent time that's past,
   and live this day as if thy last;
   improve thy talent with due care;
   for the great day thyself prepare.

3. Let all thy converse be sincere,
   thy conscience as the noon-day clear;
   think how all-seeing God thy ways
   and all thy secret thoughts surveys.

4. Wake, and lift up thyself, my heart,
   and with the angels bear thy part,
   who all night long unwearied sing
   high praise to the eternal King.

PART TWO

5. Glory to thee, who safe hast kept
   and hast refreshed me whilst I slept;
   grant, Lord, when I from death shall
     wake,
   I may of endless light partake.

6. Lord, I my vows to thee renew;
   disperse my sins as morning dew;
   guard my first springs of thought
     and will,
   and with thyself my spirit fill.

31 William James Kirkpatrick (1838-1921)

1. Away in a manger,
   no crib for a bed,
   the little Lord Jesus
   laid down his sweet head.
   The stars in the bright sky
   looked down where he lay,
   the little Lord Jesus,
   asleep on the hay.

2. The cattle are lowing,
   the baby awakes,
   but little Lord Jesus
   no crying he makes.
   I love thee, Lord Jesus!
   Look down from the sky,
   and stay by my side
   until morning is nigh.

3. Be near me Lord Jesus;
   I ask thee to stay
   close by me for ever,
   and love me, I pray.
   Bless all the dear children
   in thy tender care,
   and fit us for heaven,
   to live with thee there.

32

David J. Evans
© 1986 Thankyou Music

1. Be still, for the presence of the Lord,
   the Holy One, is here.
   Come, bow before him now,
   with reverence and fear.
   In him no sin is found,
   we stand on holy ground.
   Be still, for the presence of the Lord,
   the Holy One, is here.

2. Be still, for the glory of the Lord
   is shining all around;
   he burns with holy fire,
   with splendour he is crowned.
   How awesome is the sight,
   our radiant King of light!
   Be still, for the glory of the Lord
   is shining all around.

3. Be still, for the power of the Lord
   is moving in this place;
   he comes to cleanse and heal,
   to minister his grace.
   No work too hard for him,
   in faith receive from him.
   Be still, for the power of the Lord
   is moving in this place.

33

Katherina von Schlegel (b. 1697)
trans. Jane L. Borthwick, alt.

1. Be still, my soul: the Lord is at your side;
   bear patiently the cross of grief and pain;
   leave to your God to order and provide;
   in ev'ry change he faithful will remain.
   Be still, my soul: your best, your
     heav'nly friend,
   through thorny ways, leads to a joyful end.

2. Be still, my soul: your God will undertake
   to guide the future as he has the past.
   Your hope, your confidence let nothing
     shake,
   all now mysterious shall be clear at last.
   Be still, my soul: the tempests still obey
   his voice, who ruled them once on Galilee.

3. Be still, my soul: the hour is hastening on
   when we shall be for ever with the Lord,
   when disappointment, grief and fear
     are gone,
   sorrow forgotten, love's pure joy restored.
   Be still, my soul: when change and tears
     are past,
   all safe and blessèd we shall meet at last.

34

Isaac Williams (1802-1865)

1. Be thou my guardian and my guide,
   and hear me when I call;
   let not my slipp'ry footsteps slide,
   and hold me lest I fall.

2. The world, the flesh, and Satan dwell
   around the path I tread;
   O save me from the snares of hell,
   thou quick'ner of the dead.

3. And if I tempted am to sin,
   and outward things are strong,
   do thou, O Lord, keep watch within,
   and save my soul from wrong.

4. Still let me ever watch and pray,
   and feel that I am frail;
   that if the tempter cross my way,
   yet he may not prevail.

35

Irish 8th century, trans. Mary Byrne (1880-1931)
and Eleanor Hull (1860-1935)
© Copyright control

1. Be thou my vision, O Lord of my heart,
   naught be all else to me save that thou art;
   thou my best thought in the day and
     the night,
   waking or sleeping, thy presence my light.

2. Be thou my wisdom, be thou my
     true word,
   I ever with thee and thou with me, Lord;
   thou my great Father, and I thy true heir;
   thou in me dwelling, and I in thy care.

3. Be thou my breastplate, my sword for
      the fight,
   be thou my armour, and be thou
      my might,
   thou my soul's shelter, and thou my
      high tow'r,
   raise thou me heav'nward, O Pow'r of
      my pow'r.

4. Riches I need not, nor all the
      world's praise,
   thou mine inheritance through all my days;
   thou, and thou only, the first in my heart,
   high King of heaven, my treasure thou art!

5. High King of heaven, when battle is done,
   grant heaven's joy to me, O bright
      heav'n's sun;
   Christ of my own heart, whatever befall,
   still be my vision, O Ruler of all.

37 Frances Jane van Alstyne (Fanny J. Crosby) (1820-1915)

1. Blessed assurance, Jesus is mine:
   O what a foretaste of glory divine!
   Heir of salvation, purchase of God;
   born of his Spirit, washed in his blood.

   This is my story, this is my song,
   praising my Saviour all the day long.
   (Repeat)

2. Perfect submission, perfect delight,
   visions of rapture burst on my sight;
   angels descending, bring from above
   echoes of mercy, whispers of love.

3. Perfect submission, all is at rest,
   I in my Saviour am happy and blest;
   watching and waiting, looking above,
   filled with his goodness, lost in his love.

36 Bob Gillman
© 1977 Thankyou Music

Bind us together, Lord,
bind us together with cords
that cannot be broken.
Bind us together, Lord,
bind us together, Lord,
bind us together in love.

1. There is only one God,
   there is only one King.
   There is only one Body,
   that is why we sing:

2. Fit for the glory of God,
   purchased by his precious Blood,
   born with the right to be free:
   Jesus the vict'ry has won.

3. We are the fam'ly of God,
   we are his promise divine,
   we are his chosen desire,
   we are the glorious new wine.

38 vs 1 and 3 John Keeble (1792-1866)
vs 2 and 4 William John Hall's 'Psalms and Hymns'
(1836), alt.

1. Blest are the pure in heart,
   for they shall see our God;
   the secret of the Lord is theirs,
   their soul is Christ's abode.

2. The Lord who left the heav'ns
   our life and peace to bring,
   to dwell in lowliness with us,
   our pattern and our King.

3. Still to the lowly soul
   he doth himself impart,
   and for his dwelling and his throne
   chooseth the pure in heart.

4. Lord, we thy presence seek;
   may ours this blessing be:
   give us a pure and lowly heart,
   a temple meet for thee.

39 Josiah Conder (1789-1855)

1. Bread of heav'n, on thee we feed,
for thy flesh is meat indeed;
ever may our souls be fed
with this true and living bread;
day by day with strength supplied
through the life of him who died.

2. Vine of heav'n, thy blood supplies
this blest cup of sacrifice;
Lord, thy wounds our healing give,
to thy cross we look and live:
Jesus, may we ever be
grafted, rooted, built in thee.

40 Edwin Hatch (1835-1889), alt. the Editors
© 1999 Kevin Mayhew Ltd.

1. Breathe on me, Breath of God,
fill me with life anew,
that as you love, so may I love,
and do what you would do.

2. Breathe on me, Breath of God,
until my heart is pure:
until my will is one with yours
to do and to endure.

3. Breathe on me, Breath of God,
fulfil my heart's desire,
until this earthly part of me
glows with your heav'nly fire.

4. Breathe on me, Breath of God,
so shall I never die,
but live with you the perfect life
of your eternity.

41 Reginald Heber (1783-1826)

1. Brightest and best
of the sons of the morning,
dawn on our darkness
and lend us thine aid;
star of the east,
the horizon adorning,
guide where our infant
Redeemer is laid.

2. Cold on his cradle
the dew-drops are shining;
low lies his head
with the beasts of the stall;
angels adore him
in slumber reclining,
Maker and Monarch
and Saviour of all.

3. Say, shall we yield him,
in costly devotion,
odours of Edom,
and off'rings divine,
gems of the mountain,
and pearls of the ocean,
myrrh from the forest,
or gold from the mine?

4. Vainly we offer
each humble oblation,
vainly with gifts
would his favour secure:
richer by far
is the heart's adoration,
dearer to God
are the prayers of the poor.

42 Richard Mant (1776-1848)

1. Bright the vision that delighted
once the sight of Judah's seer;
sweet the countless tongues united
to entrance the prophet's ear.

2. Round the Lord in glory seated
cherubim and seraphim
filled his temple, and repeated
each to each the alternate hymn:

3. 'Lord, thy glory fills the heaven;
earth is with its fulness stored;
unto thee be glory given,
holy, holy, holy, Lord.'

4. Heav'n is still with glory ringing,
earth takes up the angels' cry,
'Holy, holy, holy,' singing,
'Lord of hosts, the Lord most high.'

5. With his seraph train before him,
with his holy Church below,
thus unite we to adore him,
bid we thus our anthem flow:

6. 'Lord, thy glory fills the heaven;
earth is with its fulness stored;
unto thee be glory given,
holy, holy, holy, Lord.'

43 John Byrom (1692-1763) alt.

1. Christians, awake! salute the happy morn,
whereon the Saviour of the world was
born;
rise to adore the mystery of love,
which hosts of angels chanted from
above:
with them the joyful tidings first begun
of God incarnate and the Virgin's Son.

2. Then to the watchful shepherds it was
told,
who heard th' angelic herald's voice,
'Behold,
I bring good tidings of a Saviour's birth
to you and all the nations on the earth:
this day hath God fulfilled his promised
word,
this day is born a Saviour, Christ the
Lord.'

3. He spake; and straightway the celestial
choir
in hymns of joy, unknown before,
conspire;
the praises of redeeming love they sang,
and heav'n's whole orb with alleluias
rang:
God's highest glory was their anthem
still,
peace on the earth, in ev'ry heart good
will.

4. To Bethl'em straight th'enlightened
shepherds ran,
to see, unfolding, God's eternal plan,
and found, with Joseph and the blessèd
maid,
her Son, the Saviour, in a manger laid:
then to their flocks, still praising God,
return,
and their glad hearts with holy rapture
burn.

5. O may we keep and ponder in our mind
God's wondrous love in saving lost
mankind;
trace we the babe, who hath retrieved our
loss,
from his poor manger to his bitter cross;
tread in his steps assisted by his grace,
till our first heav'nly state again takes
place.

6. Then may we hope, th'angelic hosts
among,
to sing, redeemed, a glad triumphal song:
he that was born upon this joyful day
around us all his glory shall display;
saved by his love, incessant we shall sing
eternal praise to heav'n's almighty King.

44 'Urbs beata Jerusalem', (c.7th century)
trans. John Mason Neale, (1818-1866) alt.

1. Christ is made the sure foundation,
   Christ the head and cornerstone,
   chosen of the Lord, and precious,
   binding all the Church in one,
   holy Zion's help for ever,
   and her confidence alone.

2. To this temple, where we call you,
   come, O Lord of hosts, today;
   you have promised loving kindness,
   hear your servants as we pray,
   bless your people now before you,
   turn our darkness into day.

3. Hear the cry of all your people,
   what they ask and hope to gain;
   what they gain from you, for ever
   with your chosen to retain,
   and hereafter in your glory
   evermore with you to reign.

4. Praise and honour to the Father,
   praise and honour to the Son,
   praise and honour to the Spirit,
   ever Three and ever One,
   One in might and One in glory,
   while unending ages run.

45 'Latin (before 9th century)
trans. John Chandler (1806-1876)

1. Christ is our cornerstone,
   on him alone we build;
   with his true saints alone
   the courts of heav'n are filled:
   on his great love our hopes we place
   of present grace and joys above.

2. O then with hymns of praise
   these hallowed courts shall ring;
   our voices we will raise
   the Three in One to sing;
   and thus proclaim in joyful song,
   both loud and long, that glorious name.

3. Here, gracious God, do thou
   for evermore draw nigh;
   accept each faithful vow,
   and mark each suppliant sigh;
   in copious show'r on all who pray
   each holy day thy blessings pour.

4. Here may we gain from heav'n
   the grace which we implore;
   and may that grace, once giv'n,
   be with us evermore,
   until that day when all the blest
   to endless rest are called away.

46 Michael Weisse (c. 1480-1534)
trans. Catherine Winkworth (1827-1878) alt.

1. Christ the Lord is ris'n again,
   Christ hath broken ev'ry chain.
   Hark, angelic voices cry,
   singing evermore on high,
   Alleluia.

2. He who gave for us his life,
   who for us endured the strife,
   is our paschal Lamb today;
   we too sing for joy, and say:
   Alleluia.

3. He who bore all pain and loss
   comfortless upon the cross,
   lives in glory now on high,
   pleads for us, and hears our cry:
   Alleluia.

4. He whose path no records tell,
   who descended into hell,
   who the strongest arm hath bound,
   now in highest heav'n is crowned.
   Alleluia.

5. He who slumbered in the grave
   is exalted now to save;
   now through Christendom it rings
   that the Lamb is King of kings.
   Alleluia.

6. Now he bids us tell abroad
how the lost may be restored,
how the penitent forgiv'n,
how we too may enter heav'n.
Alleluia.

7. Thou, our paschal Lamb indeed,
Christ, thy ransomed people feed;
take our sins and guilt away;
let us sing by night and day:
Alleluia.

47 Michael Saward (b. 1932)
© *Michael Saward/Jubilate Hymns*

1. Christ triumphant, ever reigning,
Saviour, Master, King.
Lord of heav'n, our lives sustaining,
hear us as we sing:

*Yours the glory and the crown,
the high renown, th'eternal name.*

2. Word incarnate, truth revealing,
Son of Man on earth!
Pow'r and majesty concealing
by your humble birth:

3. Suff'ring servant, scorned, ill-treated,
victim crucified!
Death is through the cross defeated,
sinners justified:

4. Priestly King, enthroned for ever
high in heav'n above!
Sin and death and hell shall never
stifle hymns of love:

5. So, our hearts and voices raising
through the ages long,
ceaselessly upon you gazing,
this shall be our song:

48 Charles Wesley (1707-1788)

1. Christ, whose glory fills the skies,
Christ, the true, the only light,
Sun of Righteousness arise,
triumph o'er the shades of night;
Dayspring from on high, be near;
Daystar, in my heart appear.

2. Dark and cheerless is the morn
unaccompanied by thee;
joyless is the day's return,
till thy mercy's beams I see,
till they inward light impart,
glad my eyes, and warm my heart.

3. Visit then this soul of mine,
pierce the gloom of sin and grief;
fill me, radiancy divine,
scatter all my unbelief;
more and more thyself display,
shining to the perfect day.

49 Samuel Johnson (1822-1882) alt.

1. City of God, how broad and far
outspread thy walls sublime!
Thy free and loyal people are
of ev'ry age and clime.

2. One holy Church, one mighty throng,
one steadfast, high intent;
one working band, one harvest-song,
one King omnipotent.

3. How purely hath thy speech come
down
from earth's primeval youth!
How grandly hath thine empire grown
of freedom, love and truth!

4. How gleam thy watch-fires through
the night
with never-fainting ray!
How rise thy tow'rs, serene and bright,
to meet the dawning day!

Continued overleaf

5. In vain the surge's angry shock,
   in vain the drifting sands;
   unharmed upon th'eternal Rock
   th'eternal city stands.

Sue McClellan (b. 1951), John Paculabo (b. 1946)
Keith Ryecroft (b. 1949)
© 1974 Thankyou Music

50

1. Colours of day dawn into the mind,
   the sun has come up, the night is behind.
   Go down in the city, into the street,
   and let's give the message
   to the people we meet.

   So light up the fire and let the flame burn,
   open the door, let Jesus return,
   take seeds of his Spirit, let the fruit grow,
   tell the people of Jesus, let his love show.

2. Go through the park, on into the town;
   the sun still shines on; it never goes down.
   The light of the world is risen again;
   the people of darkness
   are needing our friend.

3. Open your eyes, look into the sky,
   the darkness has come, the sun came to die.
   The evening draws on, the sun disappears,
   but Jesus is living,
   and his Spirit is near.

'Discendi, amor santo' by Bianco da Siena (d. 1434)
trans. Richard F. Littledale, (1833-1890) alt.

51

1. Come down, O Love divine,
   seek thou this soul of mine,
   and visit it with thine own ardour glowing;
   O Comforter, draw near,
   within my heart appear,
   and kindle it, thy holy flame bestowing.

2. O let it freely burn,
   till earthly passions turn
   to dust and ashes in its heat consuming;
   and let thy glorious light
   shine ever on my sight,
   and clothe me round, the while my
      path illuming.

3. Let holy charity
   mine outward vesture be,
   and lowliness become mine inner clothing;
   true lowliness of heart,
   which takes the humbler part,
   and o'er its own shortcomings weeps
      with loathing.

4. And so the yearning strong,
   with which the soul will long,
   shall far outpass the pow'r of human
      telling;
   nor can we guess its grace,
   till we become the place
   wherein the Holy Spirit makes
      his dwelling.

vs. 1-3, 5: John Cosin (1594-1672) after Rabanus Maurus
(c. 776-856) alt. v. 4: Michael Forster (b. 1946)
© v.4: 1993 Kevin Mayhew Ltd.

52

1. Come, Holy Ghost, our souls inspire,
   and lighten with celestial fire;
   thou the anointing Spirit art,
   who dost thy sev'nfold gifts impart.

2. Thy blessèd unction from above
   is comfort, life, and fire of love;
   enable with perpetual light
   the dullness of our blinded sight.

3. Anoint and cheer our soilèd face
   with the abundance of thy grace:
   keep far our foes, give peace at home;
   where thou art guide no ill can come.

4. Show us the Father and the Son,
   in thee and with thee, ever one.
   Then through the ages all along,
   this shall be our unending song.

5. 'Praise to thy eternal merit,
   Father, Son and Holy Spirit.'
   Amen.

53

Isaac Watts (1674-1748) alt.

1. Come, let us join our cheerful songs
   with angels round the throne;
   ten thousand thousand are their tongues,
   but all their joys are one.

2. 'Worthy the Lamb that died,' they cry,
   'to be exalted thus.'
   'Worthy the Lamb,' our lips reply,
   'for he was slain for us.'

3. Jesus is worthy to receive
   honour and pow'r divine;
   and blessings, more than we can give,
   be, Lord, for ever thine.

4. Let all creation join in one
   to bless the sacred name
   of him that sits upon the throne,
   and to adore the Lamb.

54

Patricia Morgan and Dave Bankhead
© 1984 Thankyou Music

Come on and celebrate
his gift of love, we will celebrate
the Son of God who loved us
and gave us life.
We'll shout your praise, O King,
you give us joy nothing else can bring;
we'll give to you our offering
in celebration praise.

Come on and celebrate, celebrate,
celebrate and sing,
celebrate and sing to the King. *(Repeat)*

55

Stephen Langton (d. 1228)
trans Edward Caswall (1814-1878) alt.

1. Come, thou Holy Spirit, come,
   and from thy celestial home
   shed a ray of light divine;
   come, thou Father of the poor,
   come, thou source of all our store,
   come, within our bosoms shine.

2. Thou of comforters the best,
   thou the soul's most welcome guest,
   sweet refreshment here below;
   in our labour rest most sweet,
   grateful coolness in the heat,
   solace in the midst of woe.

3. O most blessèd Light divine,
   shine within these hearts of thine,
   and our inmost being fill;
   where thou art not, we have naught,
   nothing good in deed or thought,
   nothing free from taint of ill.

4. Heal our wounds; our strength renew;
   on our dryness pour thy dew;
   wash the stains of guilt away;
   bend the stubborn heart and will;
   melt the frozen, warm the chill;
   guide the steps that go astray.

5. On the faithful, who adore
   and confess thee, evermore
   in thy sev'nfold gifts descend:
   give them virtue's sure reward,
   give them thy salvation, Lord,
   give them joys that never end.

56

Charles Wesley (1707-1788)

1. Come, thou long expected Jesus,
   born to set thy people free;
   from our fears and sins release us;
   let us find our rest in thee.

2. Israel's strength and consolation,
   hope of all the earth thou art;
   dear desire of ev'ry nation,
   joy of ev'ry longing heart.

3. Born thy people to deliver;
   born a child and yet a king;
   born to reign in us for ever;
   now thy gracious kingdom bring.

Continued overleaf

4. By thine own eternal Spirit,
   rule in all our hearts alone:
   by thine all-sufficient merit,
   raise us to thy glorious throne.

6. Laud and honour to the Father,
   laud and honour to the Son,
   laud and honour to the Spirit,
   ever Three and ever One,
   consubstantial, co-eternal,
   while unending ages run.

57
Job Hupton (1762-1849)
and John Mason Neale (1818-1866) alt.

1. Come, ye faithful, raise the anthem,
   cleave the skies with shouts of praise;
   sing to him who found the ransom,
   Ancient of eternal days,
   God of God, the Word incarnate,
   whom the heav'n of heav'n obeys.

2. Ere he raised the lofty mountains,
   formed the seas or built the sky,
   love eternal, free and boundless,
   moved the Lord of Life to die,
   fore-ordained the Prince of princes
   for the throne of Calvary.

3. There, for us and our redemption,
   see him all his life-blood pour!
   There he wins our full salvation,
   dies that we may die no more;
   then arising, lives for ever,
   reigning where he was before.

4. High on yon celestial mountains
   stands his sapphire throne, all bright,
   midst unending alleluias
   bursting from the saints in light;
   Sion's people tell his praises,
   victor after hard-won fight.

5. Bring your harps, and bring your
   incense,
   sweep the string and pour the lay;
   let the earth proclaim his wonders,
   King of that celestial day;
   he the Lamb once slain is worthy,
   who was dead and lives for ay.

58
St. John of Damascus (d. c. 754)
trans. John Mason Neale (1816-1866) alt.

1. Come, ye faithful, raise the strain
   of triumphant gladness:
   God hath brought his Israel
   into joy from sadness;
   loosed from Pharaoh's bitter yoke
   Jacob's sons and daughters;
   led them with unmoistened foot
   through the Red Sea waters.

2. 'Tis the spring of souls today;
   Christ hath burst his prison,
   and from three days' sleep in death
   as a sun hath risen:
   all the winter of our sins,
   long and dark, is flying
   from his light, to whom we give
   laud and praise undying.

3. Now the queen of seasons, bright
   with the day of splendour,
   with the royal feast of feasts,
   comes its joy to render;
   comes to glad Jerusalem,
   who with true affection
   welcomes in unwearied strains
   Jesu's resurrection.

4. Alleluia now we cry
   to our King immortal,
   who triumphant burst the bars
   of the tomb's dark portal;
   Alleluia, with the Son,
   God the Father praising;
   Alleluia yet again
   to the Spirit raising.

59 Henry Alford (1810-1871) alt.

1. Come, ye thankful people, come,
   raise the song of harvest-home!
   All is safely gathered in,
   ere the winter storms begin;
   God, our maker, doth provide
   for our wants to be supplied;
   come to God's own temple, come;
   raise the song of harvest-home!

2. We ourselves are God's own field,
   fruit unto his praise to yield;
   wheat and tares together sown,
   unto joy or sorrow grown;
   first the blade and then the ear,
   then the full corn shall appear:
   grant, O harvest Lord, that we
   wholesome grain and pure may be.

3. For the Lord our God shall come,
   and shall take his harvest home,
   from his field shall purge away
   all that doth offend, that day;
   give his angels charge at last
   in the fire the tares to cast,
   but the fruitful ears to store
   in his garner evermore.

4. Then, thou Church triumphant, come,
   raise the song of harvest-home;
   all be safely gathered in,
   free from sorrow, free from sin,
   there for ever purified
   in God's garner to abide:
   come, ten thousand angels, come,
   raise the glorious harvest-home!

60 Matthew Bridges (1800-1894)

1. Crown him with many crowns,
   the Lamb upon his throne;
   hark, how the heav'nly anthem drowns
   all music but its own:
   awake, my soul, and sing
   of him who died for thee,
   and hail him as thy matchless King
   through all eternity.

2. Crown him the Virgin's Son,
   the God incarnate born,
   whose arm those crimson trophies won
   which now his brow adorn;
   fruit of the mystic Rose,
   as of that Rose the Stem,
   the Root, whence mercy ever flows,
   the Babe of Bethlehem.

3. Crown him the Lord of love;
   behold his hands and side,
   rich wounds, yet visible above,
   in beauty glorified:
   no angel in the sky
   can fully bear that sight,
   but downward bends each burning eye
   at mysteries so bright.

4. Crown him the Lord of peace,
   whose pow'r a sceptre sways
   from pole to pole, that wars may cease,
   absorbed in prayer and praise:
   his reign shall know no end,
   and round his piercèd feet
   fair flow'rs of paradise extend
   their fragrance ever sweet.

5. Crown him the Lord of years,
   the Potentate of time,
   Creator of the rolling spheres,
   ineffably sublime.
   All hail, Redeemer, hail!
   for thou hast died for me;
   thy praise shall never, never fail
   throughout eternity.

61

John Greenleaf Whittier (1807-1892)

1. Dear Lord and Father of mankind,
   forgive our foolish ways!
   Re-clothe us in our rightful mind,
   in purer lives thy service find,
   in deeper rev'rence praise,
   in deeper rev'rence praise.

2. In simple trust like theirs who heard,
   beside the Syrian sea,
   the gracious calling of the Lord,
   let us, like them, without a word,
   rise up and follow thee,
   rise up and follow thee.

3. O Sabbath rest by Galilee!
   O calm of hills above,
   where Jesus knelt to share with thee
   the silence of eternity,
   interpreted by love!
   Interpreted by love!

4. Drop thy still dews of quietness,
   till all our strivings cease;
   take from our souls the strain and stress,
   and let our ordered lives confess
   the beauty of thy peace,
   the beauty of thy peace.

5. Breathe through the heats of our desire
   thy coolness and thy balm;
   let sense be dumb, let flesh retire;
   speak through the earthquake,
      wind and fire,
   O still small voice of calm!
   O still small voice of calm!

62

Ratcliffe Woodward (1848-1934) © SPCK

1. Ding dong, merrily on high!
   In heav'n the bells are ringing;
   ding dong, verily the sky
   is riv'n with angel singing.

Gloria, hosanna in excelsis!
Gloria, hosanna in excelsis!

2. E'en so here below, below,
   let steeple bells be swungen,
   and io, io, io,
   by priest and people sungen.

3. Pray you, dutifully prime
   your matin chime, ye ringers;
   may you beautifully rhyme
   your evetime song, ye singers.

63

J. B. de Santeuil (1630-1697)
trans. Isaac Williams (1802-1865) alt.

1. Disposer supreme,
   and Judge of the earth,
   thou choosest for thine
   the meek and the poor;
   to frail earthen vessels,
   and things of no worth,
   entrusting thy riches
   which ay shall endure.

2. Those vessels are frail,
   though full of thy light,
   and many, once made,
   are broken and gone;
   thence brightly appeareth
   thy truth in its might,
   as through the clouds riven
   the lightnings have shone.

3. Like clouds are they borne
   to do thy great will,
   and swift as the winds
   about the world go:
   the Word with his wisdom
   their spirits doth fill;
   they thunder, they lighten,
   the waters o'erflow.

4. Their sound goeth forth,
   'Christ Jesus the Lord!'
   then Satan doth fear,
   his citadels fall;
   as when the dread trumpets
   went forth at thy word,
   and one long blast shattered
   the Canaanites' wall.

5. O loud be their cry,
   and stirring their sound,
   to rouse us, O Lord,
   from slumber of sin:
   the lights thou hast kindled
   in darkness around,
   O may they awaken
   our spirits within.

6. All honour and praise,
   dominion and might,
   to God, Three in One,
   eternally be,
   who round us hath shed
   his own marvellous light,
   and called us from darkness
   his glory to see.

64

Gerard Markland (b. 1953), based on Isaiah 43:1-4
© 1978 Kevin Mayhew Ltd.

Do not be afraid, for I have redeemed you.
I have called you by your name;
you are mine.

1. When you walk through the waters,
   I'll be with you.
   You will never sink beneath the waves.

2. When the fire is burning
   all around you,
   you will never be consumed by the flames.

3. When the fear of loneliness
   is looming,
   then remember I am at your side.

4. When you dwell in the exile
   of the stranger,
   remember you are precious in my eyes.

5. You are mine, O my child,
   I am your Father,
   and I love you with a perfect love.

65

William Whiting (1825-1878), alt.

1. Eternal Father, strong to save,
   whose arm doth bind the restless wave,
   who bidd'st the mighty ocean deep
   its own appointed limits keep:
   O hear us when we cry to thee
   for those in peril on the sea.

2. O Saviour, whose almighty word
   the winds and waves submissive heard,
   who walkedst on the foaming deep,
   and calm, amid its rage, didst sleep:
   O hear us when we cry to thee
   for those in peril on the sea.

3. O sacred Spirit, who didst brood
   upon the waters dark and rude,
   and bid their angry tumult cease,
   and give, for wild confusion, peace:
   O hear us when we cry to thee
   for those in peril on the sea.

4. O Trinity of love and pow'r,
   our brethren shield in danger's hour.
   From rock and tempest, fire and foe,
   protect them whereso'er they go,
   and ever let there rise to thee
   glad hymns of praise from land and sea.

66

Thomas Benson Pollock (1836-1896)

1. Faithful Shepherd, feed me
   in the pastures green;
   faithful Shepherd, lead me
   where thy steps are seen.

Continued overleaf

2. Hold me fast, and guide me
in the narrow way;
so, with thee beside me,
I shall never stray.

3. Daily bring me nearer
to the heav'nly shore;
may my faith grow clearer,
may I love thee more.

4. Hallow ev'ry pleasure,
ev'ry gift and pain;
be thyself my treasure,
though none else I gain.

5. Day by day prepare me
as thou seest best,
then let angels bear me
to thy promised rest.

67 Maria Willis (1824-1908)

1. Father, hear the prayer we offer:
not for ease that prayer shall be,
but for strength that we may ever
live our lives courageously.

2. Not for ever in green pastures
do we ask our way to be;
but the steep and rugged pathway
may we tread rejoicingly.

3. Not for ever by still waters
would we idly rest and stay;
but would smite the living fountains
from the rocks along our way.

4. Be our strength in hours of weakness,
in our wand'rings be our guide;
through endeavour, failure, danger,
Father, be thou at our side.

68 Jenny Hewer (b. 1945)
© 1975 Thankyou Music

1. Father, I place into your hands
the things I cannot do.
Father, I place into your hands
the things that I've been through.
Father, I place into your hands
the way that I should go,
for I know I always can trust you.

2. Father, I place into your hands
my friends and family.
Father, I place into your hands
the things that trouble me.
Father I place into your hands
the person I would be,
for I know I always can trust you.

3. Father, we love to see your face,
we love to hear your voice,
Father, we love to sing your praise
and in your name rejoice.
Father, we love to walk with you
and in your presence rest,
for we know we always can trust you.

4. Father, I want to be with you
and do the things you do.
Father, I want to speak the words
that you are speaking too.
Father, I want to love the ones
that you will draw to you,
for I know that I am one with you.

69 Edward Cooper (1770-1833)

1. Father of heav'n, whose love profound
a ransom for our souls hath found,
before thy throne we sinners bend,
to us thy pard'ning love extend.

2. Almighty Son, incarnate Word,
our Prophet, Priest, Redeemer, Lord,
before thy throne we sinners bend,
to us thy saving grace extend.

3. Eternal Spirit, by whose breath
the soul is raised from sin and death,
before thy throne we sinners bend,
to us thy quick'ning pow'r extend.

4. Thrice Holy! Father, Spirit, Son;
mysterious Godhead, Three in One,
before thy throne we sinners bend,
grace, pardon, life, to us extend.

70
Terrye Coelho (b. 1952)
© 1972 Maranatha! Music. Administered by CopyCare

1. Father, we adore you,
lay our lives before you.
How we love you!

2. Jesus, we adore you . . .

3. Spirit, we adore you . . .

71
Donna Adkins (b. 1940)
© 1976 Maranatha! Music. Administered by CopyCare

1. Father, we love you,
we worship and adore you,
glorify your name in all the earth.
Glorify your name, glorify your name,
glorify your name in all the earth.

2. Jesus, we love you . . .

3. Spirit, we love you . . .

72
John Samuel Bewley Monsell (1811-1875), alt.

1. Fight the good fight with all thy might;
Christ is thy strength, and Christ thy right;
lay hold on life, and it shall be
thy joy and crown eternally.

2. Run the straight race through God's
good grace,
lift up thine eyes and seek his face;
life with its way before us lies;
Christ is the path, and Christ the prize.

3. Cast care aside, lean on thy guide;
his boundless mercy will provide;
trust, and thy trusting soul shall prove
Christ is its life, and Christ its love.

4. Faint not nor fear, his arms are near;
he changeth not, and thou art dear;
only believe, and thou shalt see
that Christ is all in all to thee.

73
Timothy Dudley-Smith (b. 1926)
© Timothy Dudley-Smith

1. Fill your hearts with joy and gladness,
sing and praise your God and mine!
Great the Lord in love and wisdom,
might and majesty divine!
He who framed the starry heavens
knows and names them as they shine.
Fill your hearts with joy and gladness,
sing and praise your God and mine!

2. Praise the Lord, his people, praise him!
Wounded souls his comfort know.
Those who fear him find his mercies,
peace for pain and joy for woe;
humble hearts are high exalted,
human pride and pow'r laid low.
Praise the Lord, his people, praise him!
Wounded souls his comfort know.

3. Praise the Lord for times and seasons,
cloud and sunshine, wind and rain;
spring to melt the snows of winter
till the waters flow again;
grass upon the mountain pastures,
golden valleys thick with grain.
Praise the Lord for times and seasons,
cloud and sunshine, wind and rain.

4. Fill your hearts with joy and gladness,
peace and plenty crown your days!
Love his laws, declare his judgements,
walk in all his words and ways;
he the Lord and we his children,
praise the Lord, all people, praise!
Fill your hearts with joy and gladness,
peace and plenty crown your days!

74

John Henry Newman (1801-1890) alt.

1. Firmly I believe and truly
   God is Three and God is One;
   and I next acknowledge duly
   manhood taken by the Son.

2. And I trust and hope most fully
   in the Saviour crucified;
   and each thought and deed unruly
   do to death as he has died.

3. Simply to his grace and wholly
   light and life and strength belong,
   and I love supremely, solely,
   him the holy, him the strong.

4. And I hold in veneration,
   for the love of him alone,
   holy Church as his creation,
   and her teachings as his own.

5. Adoration ay be given,
   with and thro' th'angelic host,
   to the God of earth and heaven,
   Father, Son and Holy Ghost.

   *When the tune 'Alton' is used the following
   last line is added:*
   Amen. Father, Son and Holy Ghost.

75

William Walsham How (1823-1897)

1. For all the saints
   who from their labours rest,
   who thee by faith
   before the world confessed,
   thy name, O Jesus,
   be for ever blest.

   Alleluia, alleluia!

2. Thou wast their rock,
   their fortress and their might;
   thou, Lord, their captain
   in the well-fought fight;
   thou in the darkness drear
   their one true light.

3. O may thy soldiers,
   faithful, true and bold,
   fight as the saints
   who nobly fought of old,
   and win, with them,
   the victor's crown of gold.

4. O blest communion!
   fellowship divine!
   we feebly struggle,
   they in glory shine;
   yet all are one in thee,
   for all are thine.

5. And when the strife is fierce,
   the warfare long,
   steals on the ear
   the distant triumph song,
   and hearts are brave again,
   and arms are strong.

6. The golden evening
   brightens in the west;
   soon, soon to faithful
   warriors cometh rest;
   sweet is the calm of
   paradise the blest.

7. But lo! There breaks
   a yet more glorious day;
   the saints triumphant
   rise in bright array:
   the King of glory
   passes on his way.

8. From earth's wide bounds,
   from ocean's farthest coast,
   through gates of pearl
   streams in the countless host,
   singing to Father,
   Son and Holy Ghost.

76

Folliot Sandford Pierpoint (1835-1917)

1. For the beauty of the earth,
   for the beauty of the skies,
   for the love which from our birth
   over and around us lies:

   Lord of all, to thee we raise
   this our sacrifice of praise.

2. For the beauty of each hour
   of the day and of the night,
   hill and vale and tree and flow'r,
   sun and moon and stars of light:

3. For the joy of human love,
   brother, sister, parent, child,
   friends on earth, and friends above,
   pleasures pure and undefiled:

4. For each perfect gift of thine,
   to our race so freely giv'n,
   graces human and divine,
   flow'rs of earth and buds of heav'n:

5. For thy Church which evermore
   lifteth holy hands above,
   off'ring up on ev'ry shore
   her pure sacrifice of love:

77

George Hunt Smyttan (1822-1870)
adapted by Michael Forster (b. 1946)
© 1999 Kevin Mayhew Ltd.

1. Forty days and forty nights
   you were fasting in the wild;
   forty days and forty nights,
   tempted still, yet unbeguiled.

2. Sunbeams scorching all the day,
   chilly dew-drops nightly shed,
   prowling beasts about your way,
   stones your pillow, earth your bed.

3. Let us your endurance share,
   and from earthly greed abstain,
   with you vigilant in prayer,
   with you strong to suffer pain.

4. Then if evil on us press,
   flesh or spirit to assail,
   Victor in the wilderness,
   help us not to swerve or fail.

5. So shall peace divine be ours;
   holy gladness, pure and true:
   come to us, angelic powers,
   such as ministered to you.

6. Keep, O keep us, Saviour dear,
   ever constant by your side,
   that with you we may appear
   at th'eternal Eastertide.

78

Graham Kendrick (b. 1950)
© 1983 Thankyou Music

1. From heav'n you came, helpless babe,
   entered our world, your glory veiled;
   not to be served but to serve,
   and give your life that we might live.

   This is our God, the Servant King,
   he calls us now to follow him,
   to bring our lives as a daily offering
   of worship to the Servant King.

2. There in the garden of tears,
   my heavy load he chose to bear;
   his heart with sorrow was torn.
   'Yet not my will but yours,' he said.

3. Come see his hands and his feet,
   the scars that speak of sacrifice,
   hands that flung stars into space,
   to cruel nails surrendered.

4. So let us learn how to serve,
   and in our lives enthrone him;
   each other's needs to prefer,
   for it is Christ we're serving.

79 Traditional

1. Give me joy in my heart, keep me praising,
   give me joy in my heart, I pray.
   Give me joy in my heart, keep my praising,
   keep me praising till the end of day.

   Sing hosanna! Sing hosanna!
   Sing hosanna to the King of kings!
   Sing hosanna! Sing hosanna!
   Sing hosanna to the King!

2. Give me peace in my heart,
   keep me resting . . .

3. Give me love in my heart,
   keep me serving . . .

4. Give me oil in my lamp,
   keep me burning . . .

80 Henry Smith. © 1978 Integrity's Hosanna! Music/ Sovereign Music UK

Give thanks with a grateful heart,
give thanks to the Holy One,
give thanks because he's given
Jesus Christ, his Son.
And now let the weak say, 'I am strong',
let the poor say, 'I am rich',
because of what the Lord has done for us.
And now let the weak say, 'I am strong',
let the poor say, 'I am rich',
because of what the Lord has done for us.

81 John Newton (1725-1807) based on Isaiah 33:20-21, alt.

1. Glorious things of thee are spoken,
   Zion, city of our God;
   he whose word cannot be broken
   formed thee for his own abode.
   On the Rock of Ages founded,
   what can shake thy sure repose?
   With salvation's walls surrounded,
   thou may'st smile at all thy foes.

2. See, the streams of living waters,
   springing from eternal love,
   well supply thy sons and daughters,
   and all fear of want remove.
   Who can faint while such a river
   ever flows their thirst to assuage?
   Grace which, like the Lord, the giver,
   never fails from age to age.

3. Round each habitation hov'ring,
   see the cloud and fire appear
   for a glory and a cov'ring,
   showing that the Lord is near.
   Thus they march, the pillar leading,
   light by night and shade by day;
   daily on the manna feeding
   which he gives them when they pray.

4. Saviour, if of Zion's city
   I through grace a member am,
   let the world deride or pity,
   I will glory in thy name.
   Fading is the worldling's pleasure,
   boasted pomp and empty show;
   solid joys and lasting treasure
   none but Zion's children know.

82 Book of Hours (1514)

God be in my head,
and in my understanding;
God be in mine eyes,
and in my looking;
God be in my mouth,
and in my speaking;
God be in my heart,
and in my thinking;
God be at mine end,
and at my departing.

83

Percy Dearmer (1867-1936) alt.
© Oxford University Press

1. God is love: his the care,
   tending each, ev'rywhere.
   God is love, all is there!
   Jesus came to show him,
   that we all might know him!

   Sing aloud, loud, loud!
   Sing aloud, loud, loud!
   God is good! God is truth!
   God is beauty! Praise him!

2. None can see God above;
   we can share life and love;
   thus may we Godward move,
   seek him in creation,
   holding ev'ry nation.

3. Jesus lived on the earth,
   hope and life brought to birth
   and affirmed human worth,
   for he came to save us
   by the truth he gave us.

4. To our Lord praise we sing,
   light and life, friend and King,
   coming down, love to bring,
   pattern for our duty,
   showing God in beauty.

84

William Cowper (1731-1800)

1. God moves in a mysterious way
   his wonders to perform;
   he plants his footsteps in the sea,
   and rides upon the storm.

2. Deep in unfathomable mines
   of never-failing skill,
   he treasures up his bright designs,
   and works his sov'reign will.

3. Ye fearful saints, fresh courage take;
   the clouds ye so much dread
   are big with mercy, and shall break
   in blessings on your head.

4. Judge not the Lord by feeble sense,
   but trust him for his grace;
   behind a frowning providence
   he hides a shining face.

5. His purposes will ripen fast,
   unfolding ev'ry hour;
   the bud may have a bitter taste,
   but sweet will be the flow'r.

6. Blind unbelief is sure to err,
   and scan his work in vain;
   God is his own interpreter,
   and he will make it plain.

85

Henry Francis Lyte (1793-1847)
based on Psalm 67, alt.

1. God of mercy, God of grace,
   show the brightness of thy face;
   shine upon us, Saviour, shine,
   fill thy Church with light divine;
   and thy saving health extend
   unto earth's remotest end.

2. Let the people praise thee, Lord;
   be by all that live adored;
   let the nations shout and sing
   glory to their Saviour King;
   at thy feet their tribute pay,
   and thy holy will obey.

3. Let the people praise thee, Lord;
   earth shall then her fruits afford;
   God to us his blessing give,
   we to God devoted live;
   all below, and all above,
   one in joy and light and love.

86

Alan Dale and Hubert J. Richards (b. 1921)
© 1982 Kevin Mayhew Ltd.

1. God's Spirit is in my heart.
   He has called me and set me apart.
   This is what I have to do,
   what I have to do.

Continued overleaf

He sent me to give
the Good News to the poor,
tell pris'ners that they are pris'ners no more,
tell blind people that they can see,
and set the down trodden free,
and go tell ev'ry one the news
that the kingdom of God has come,
and go tell ev'ryone the news
that God's kingdom has come.

2. Just as the Father sent me,
   so I'm sending you out to be
   my witnesses throughout the world,
   the whole of the world.

3. Don't carry a load in your pack,
   you don't need two shirts on your back.
   A workman can earn his own keep,
   can earn his own keep.

4. Don't worry what you have to say,
   don't worry because on that day
   God's Spirit will speak in your heart,
   will speak in your heart.

87 James Edward Seddon (1915-1983)
© Mrs. M. Seddon/Jubilee Hymns

1. Go forth and tell!
   O Church of God, awake!
   God's saving news
   to all the nations take:
   proclaim Christ Jesus,
   Saviour, Lord and King,
   that all the world
   his worthy praise may sing.

2. Go forth and tell!
   God's love embraces all;
   he will in grace
   respond to all who call;
   how shall they call
   if they have never heard
   the gracious invitation
   of his word?

3. Go forth and tell!
   where still the darkness lies;
   in wealth or want,
   the sinner surely dies:
   give us, O Lord,
   concern of heart and mind,
   a love like yours
   which cares for all mankind.

4. Go forth and tell!
   the doors are open wide:
   share God's good gifts –
   let no-one be denied;
   live out your life
   as Christ your Lord shall choose,
   your ransomed pow'rs
   for his sole glory use.

5. Go forth and tell!
   O Church of God, arise!
   Go in the strength
   which Christ your Lord supplies;
   go till all nations
   his great name adore
   and serve him, Lord and King,
   for evermore.

88 John Mason Neale (1818-1866) alt.

1. Good King Wenceslas looked out
   on the feast of Stephen,
   when the snow lay round about,
   deep, and crisp, and even;
   brightly shone the moon that night,
   though the frost was cruel,
   when a poor man came in sight,
   gath'ring winter fuel.

2. 'Hither, page, and stand by me,
   if thou know'st it, telling,
   yonder peasant, who is he,
   where and what his dwelling?'
   'Sire, he lives a good league hence,
   underneath the mountain,
   right against the forest fence,
   by Saint Agnes' fountain.'

3. 'Bring me flesh, and bring me wine,
   bring me pine logs hither:
   thou and I will see him dine,
   when we bring him thither.'
   Page and monarch, forth they went,
   forth they went together;
   through the rude wind's wild lament,
   and the bitter weather.

4. 'Sire, the night is darker now,
   and the wind blows stronger;
   fails my heart, I know not how;
   I can go no longer.'
   'Mark my footsteps good, my page;
   tread thou in them boldly:
   thou shalt find the winter's rage
   freeze thy blood less coldly.'

5. In his master's steps he trod,
   where the snow lay dinted;
   heat was in the very sod
   which the Saint had printed.
   Therefore, Christians all, be sure,
   wealth or rank possessing,
   ye who now will bless the poor,
   shall yourselves find blessing.

89 Thomas Obadiah Chisholm (1866-1960)
   © 1951 Hope Publishing Co. Administered by CopyCare

1. Great is thy faithfulness,
   O God my Father,
   there is no shadow
   of turning with thee;
   thou changest not,
   thy compassions, they fail not;
   as thou hast been
   thou for ever wilt be.

   Great is thy faithfulness!
   Great is thy faithfulness!
   Morning by morning
   new mercies I see;
   all I have needed
   thy hand hath provided,
   great is thy faithfulness,
   Lord, unto me!

2. Summer and winter,
   and springtime and harvest,
   sun, moon and stars
   in their courses above,
   join with all nature
   in manifold witness
   to thy great faithfulness,
   mercy and love.

3. Pardon for sin
   and a peace that endureth,
   thine own dear presence
   to cheer and to guide;
   strength for today
   and bright hope for tomorrow,
   blessings all mine,
   with ten thousand beside!

90 William Williams (1717-1791)
   trans. Peter Williams (1727-1796) and others

1. Guide me, O thou great Redeemer,
   pilgrim through this barren land;
   I am weak, but thou art mighty,
   hold me with thy pow'rful hand:
   Bread of Heaven, Bread of Heaven,
   feed me till I want no more,
   feed me till I want no more.

2. Open now the crystal fountain,
   whence the healing stream doth flow;
   let the fire and cloudy pillar
   lead me all my journey through;
   strong deliv'rer, strong deliv'rer,
   be thou still my strength and shield,
   be thou still my strength and shield.

3. When I tread the verge of Jordan,
   bid my anxious fears subside;
   death of death, and hell's destruction,
   land me safe on Canaan's side;
   songs of praises, songs of praises,
   I will ever give to thee,
   I will ever give to thee.

91

Charles Wesley (1707-1788)
Thomas Cotterill (1779-1823) and others, alt.

1. Hail the day that sees him rise, *alleluia!*
   to his throne above the skies; *alleluia!*
   Christ the Lamb, for sinners giv'n, *alleluia!*
   enters now the highest heav'n! *alleluia!*

2. There for him high triumph waits;
   lift your heads, eternal gates!
   He hath conquered death and sin;
   take the King of Glory in!

3. Circled round with angel-pow'rs,
   their triumphant Lord and ours;
   wide unfold the radiant scene,
   take the King of Glory in!

4. Lo, the heav'n its Lord receives,
   yet he loves the earth he leaves;
   though returning to his throne,
   calls the human race his own.

5. See, he lifts his hands above;
   see, he shows the prints of love;
   hark, his gracious lips bestow
   blessings on his Church below.

6. Still for us he intercedes,
   his prevailing death he pleads;
   near himself prepares our place,
   he the first-fruits of our race.

7. Lord, though parted from our sight,
   far above the starry height,
   grant our hearts may thither rise,
   seeking thee above the skies.

8. Ever upward let us move,
   wafted on the wings of love;
   looking when our Lord shall come,
   longing, sighing after home.

92

Paraphrase of Psalm 71 by James Montgomery
(1771-1854)

1. Hail to the Lord's anointed,
   great David's greater son!
   Hail, in the time appointed,
   his reign on earth begun!
   He comes to break oppression,
   to set the captive free;
   to take away transgression,
   and rule in equity.

2. He comes with succour speedy
   to those who suffer wrong;
   to help the poor and needy,
   and bid the weak be strong;
   to give them songs for sighing,
   their darkness turn to light,
   whose souls, condemned and dying,
   were precious in his sight.

3. He shall come down like showers
   upon the fruitful earth,
   and love, joy, hope, like flowers,
   spring in his path to birth:
   before him on the mountains
   shall peace the herald go;
   and righteousness in fountains
   from hill to valley flow.

4. Kings shall fall down before him,
   and gold and incense bring;
   all nations shall adore him,
   his praise all people sing;
   to him shall prayer unceasing
   and daily vows ascend;
   his kingdom still increasing,
   a kingdom without end.

5. O'er ev'ry foe victorious,
   he on his throne shall rest,
   from age to age more glorious,
   all-blessing and all-blest;
   the tide of time shall never
   his covenant remove;
   his name shall stand for ever;
   that name to us is love.

93

Tim Cullen, alt.
© 1975 Celebration/Kingsway Music

Hallelujah, my Father,
for giving us your Son;
sending him into the world
to be given up for all,
knowing we would bruise him
and smite him from the earth!
Hallelujah, my Father,
in his death is my birth.
Hallelujah, my Father,
in his life is my life.

94

'Vox clara ecce intonat' 6th century,
trans. Edward Caswall (1814-1878)

1. Hark! a herald voice is calling:
   'Christ is nigh!' it seems to say;
   'Cast away the dreams of darkness,
   O ye children of the day!'

2. Startled at the solemn warning,
   let the earth-bound soul arise;
   Christ, her sun, all sloth dispelling,
   shines upon the morning skies.

3. Lo, the Lamb, so long expected,
   comes with pardon down from heav'n;
   let us haste, with tears of sorrow,
   one and all to be forgiv'n.

4. So when next he comes with glory,
   wrapping all the earth in fear,
   may he then, as our defender,
   on the clouds of heav'n appear.

5. Honour, glory, virtue, merit,
   to the Father and the Son,
   with the co-eternal Spirit,
   while unending ages run.

95

Philip Doddridge (1702-1751) based on Luke 4:18-19

1. Hark the glad sound! the Saviour comes,
   the Saviour promised long:
   let ev'ry heart prepare a throne,
   and ev'ry voice a song.

2. He comes, the pris'ners to release
   in Satan's bondage held;
   the gates of brass before him burst,
   the iron fetters yield.

3. He comes, the broken heart to bind,
   the bleeding soul to cure,
   and with the treasures of his grace
   to bless the humble poor.

4. Our glad hosannas, Prince of Peace,
   thy welcome shall proclaim;
   and heav'n's eternal arches ring
   with thy belovèd name.

96

Charles Wesley (1707-1788), George Whitefield (1714-1770), Martin Madan (1726-1790) and others, alt.

1. Hark, the herald-angels sing
   glory to the new-born King;
   peace on earth and mercy mild,
   God and sinners reconciled:
   joyful, all ye nations rise,
   join the triumph of the skies,
   with th'angelic host proclaim,
   'Christ is born in Bethlehem.'

   Hark, the herald-angels sing
   glory to the new-born King.

2. Christ, by highest heav'n adored,
   Christ, the everlasting Lord,
   late in time behold him come,
   offspring of a virgin's womb!
   Veiled in flesh the Godhead see,
   hail, th'incarnate Deity!
   Pleased as man with us to dwell,
   Jesus, our Emmanuel.

3. Hail, the heav'n-born Prince of Peace!
   Hail, the Sun of Righteousness!
   Light and life to all he brings,
   ris'n with healing in his wings;
   mild he lays his glory by,
   born that we no more may die,
   born to raise us from the earth,
   born to give us second birth.

97

Percy Dearmer (1867-1936)
after John Bunyan (1628-1688) © *Oxford University Press*

1. He who would valiant be
'gainst all disaster,
let him in constancy
follow the Master.
There's no discouragement
shall make him once relent
his first avowed intent
to be a pilgrim.

2. Who so beset him round
with dismal stories,
do but themselves confound –
his strength the more is.
No foes shall stay his might,
though he with giants fight:
he will make good his right
to be a pilgrim.

3. Since, Lord, thou dost defend
us with thy Spirit,
we know we at the end
shall life inherit.
Then fancies flee away!
I'll fear not what men say,
I'll labour night and day
to be a pilgrim.

98

Charles Edward Oakley (1832-1865), adapted

1. Hills of the north, rejoice,
echoing songs arise,
hail with united voice
him who made earth and skies:
he comes in righteousness and love,
he brings salvation from above.

2. Isles of the southern seas
sing to the list'ning earth,
carry on ev'ry breeze
hope of a world's new birth:
in Christ shall all be made anew,
his word is sure, his promise true.

3. Lands of the east, arise,
he is your brightest morn,
greet him with joyous eyes,
praise shall his path adorn:
the God whom you have longed to know
in Christ draws near, and calls you now.

4. Shores of the utmost west,
lands of the setting sun,
welcome the heav'nly guest
in whom the dawn has come:
he brings a never-ending light
who triumphed o'er our darkest night.

5. Shout, as you journey on,
songs be in ev'ry mouth,
lo, from the north they come,
from east and west and south:
in Jesus all shall find their rest,
in him the longing earth be blest.

99

Reginald Heber (1783-1826)

1. Holy, holy, holy!
Lord God almighty!
Early in the morning
our song shall rise to thee;
holy, holy, holy!
Merciful and mighty!
God in three persons,
blessed Trinity!

2.* Holy, holy, holy!
All the saints adore thee,
casting down their golden crowns
around the glassy sea;
cherubim and seraphim
falling down before thee,
which wert, and art,
and evermore shall be.

3. Holy, holy, holy!
   Though the darkness hide thee,
   though the sinful mortal eye
   thy glory may not see,
   only thou art holy,
   there is none beside thee,
   perfect in pow'r,
   in love, and purity.

4. Holy, holy, holy!
   Lord God almighty!
   All thy works shall praise thy name,
   in earth and sky and sea;
   holy, holy, holy!
   Merciful and mighty!
   God in three persons,
   blessèd Trinity!
   * May be omitted

100

Carl Tuttle
© 1985 Mercy/Vineyard Publishing
Administered by CopyCare

1. Hosanna, hosanna,
   hosanna in the highest! *(Repeat)*

   Lord, we lift up your name,
   with hearts full of praise;
   be exalted, O Lord, my God!
   Hosanna in the highest!

2. Glory, glory, glory
   to the King of kings! *(Repeat)*

101

Stuart Townend
© 1995 Thankyou Music

1. How deep the Father's love for us,
   how vast beyond all measure,
   that he should give his only Son
   to make a wretch his treasure.
   How great the pain of searing loss,
   the Father turns his face away,
   as wounds which mar the Chosen One
   bring many sons to glory.

2. Behold the man upon a cross,
   my sin upon his shoulders;
   ashamed, I hear my mocking voice
   call out among the scoffers.
   It was my sin that held him there
   until it was accomplished;
   his dying breath has brought me life –
   I know that it is finished.

3. I will not boast in anything,
   no gifts, no pow'r, no wisdom;
   but I will boast in Jesus Christ,
   his death and resurrection.
   Why should I gain from his reward?
   I cannot give an answer,
   but this I know with all my heart,
   his wounds have paid my ransom.

102 Richard Keen (c. 1787)

1. How firm a foundation,
   ye saints of the Lord,
   is laid for your faith
   in his excellent word;
   what more can he say
   than to you he hath said,
   you who unto Jesus
   for refuge have fled?

2. Fear not, he is with thee,
   O be not dismayed;
   for he is thy God,
   and will still give thee aid:
   he'll strengthen thee, help thee,
   and cause thee to stand,
   upheld by his righteous,
   omnipotent hand.

3. In ev'ry condition,
   in sickness, in health,
   in poverty's vale,
   or abounding in wealth;
   at home and abroad,
   on the land, on the sea,
   as thy days may demand
   shall thy strength ever be.

Continued overleaf

4. When through the deep waters
he calls thee to go,
the rivers of grief
shall not thee overflow;
for he will be with thee
in trouble to bless,
and sanctify to thee
thy deepest distress.

5. When through fiery trials
thy pathway shall lie,
his grace all-sufficient
shall be thy supply;
the flame shall not hurt thee,
his only design
thy dross to consume
and thy gold to refine.

6. The soul that on Jesus
has leaned for repose
he will not, he cannot,
desert to its foes;
that soul, though all hell
should endeavour to shake,
he never will leave,
he will never forsake.

103

v 1 Leonard E. Smith Jnr (b. 1942)
based on Isaiah 52:7-10 vs 2-4 unknown.
© 1974 Thankyou Music

1. How lovely on the mountains
are the feet of him
who brings good news, good news,
announcing peace,
proclaiming news of happiness:
our God reigns, our God reigns.

Our God reigns. (x4)

2. You watchmen, lift your voices
joyfully as one,
shout for your King, your King!
See eye to eye,
the Lord restoring Zion:
our God reigns, our God reigns.

3. Wasteplaces of Jerusalem,
break forth with joy!
We are redeemed, redeemed.
The Lord has saved
and comforted his people:
our God reigns, our God reigns.

4. Ends of the earth, see
the salvation of our God!
Jesus is Lord, is Lord!
Before the nations,
he has bared his holy arm:
our God reigns, our God reigns.

104 John Newton (1725-1807)

1. How sweet the name of Jesus sounds
in a believer's ear!
It soothes our sorrows, heals our
wounds,
and drives away our fear.

2. It makes the wounded spirit whole,
and calms the troubled breast;
'tis manna to the hungry soul,
and to the weary rest.

3. Dear name! the rock on which I build,
my shield and hiding-place,
my never-failing treas'ry filled
with boundless stores of grace.

4. Jesus! my shepherd, brother, friend,
my prophet, priest, and king,
my Lord, my life, my way, my end,
accept the praise I bring.

5. Weak is the effort of my heart,
and cold my warmest thought;
but when I see thee as thou art,
I'll praise thee as I ought.

6. Till then I would thy love proclaim
with ev'ry fleeting breath;
and may the music of thy name
refresh my soul in death.

105

Dave Bilbrough
© 1983 Thankyou Music

I am a new creation,
no more in condemnation,
here in the grace of God I stand.
My heart is overflowing,
my love just keeps on growing,
here in the grace of God I stand.

And I will praise you, Lord,
yes, I will praise you, Lord,
and I will sing of all that you have done.
A joy that knows no limit,
a lightness in my spirit,
here in the grace of God I stand.

106

William Young Fullerton (1857-1932), alt.
© Copyright control

1. I cannot tell
   how he whom angels worship
   should stoop to love
   the peoples of the earth,
   or why as shepherd
   he should seek the wand'rer
   with his mysterious promise
   of new birth.
   But this I know,
   that he was born of Mary,
   when Bethl'em's manger
   was his only home,
   and that he lived at
   Nazareth and laboured,
   and so the Saviour,
   Saviour of the world, is come.

2. I cannot tell
   how silently he suffered,
   as with his peace
   he graced this place of tears,
   or how his heart
   upon the cross was broken,
   the crown of pain
   to three and thirty years.
   But this I know,
   he heals the broken-hearted,
   and stays our sin,
   and calms our lurking fear,
   and lifts the burden
   from the heavy laden,
   for yet the Saviour,
   Saviour of the world, is here.

3. I cannot tell
   how he will win the nations,
   how he will claim
   his earthly heritage,
   how satisfy
   the needs and aspirations
   of east and west,
   of sinner and of sage.
   But this I know,
   all flesh shall see his glory,
   and he shall reap
   the harvest he has sown,
   and some glad day
   his sun shall shine in splendour
   when he the Saviour,
   Saviour of the world, is known.

4. I cannot tell
   how all the lands shall worship,
   when, at his bidding,
   ev'ry storm is stilled,
   or who can say
   how great the jubilation
   when ev'ry heart
   with perfect love is filled.
   But this I know,
   the skies will thrill with rapture,
   and myriad, myriad
   human voices sing,
   and earth to heav'n,
   and heav'n to earth, will answer:
   'At last the Saviour,
   Saviour of the world, is King!'

107

Sydney Carter (b. 1915)
© 1963 Stainer & Bell Ltd.

1. I danced in the morning
when the world was begun,
and I danced in the moon
and the stars and the sun,
and I came down from heaven
and I danced on the earth,
at Bethlehem I had my birth.

Dance then, wherever you may be,
I am the Lord of the Dance, said he,
and I'll lead you all, wherever you may be,
and I'll lead you all in the dance, said he.

2. I danced for the scribe
and the Pharisee,
but they would not dance
and they wouldn't follow me.
I danced for the fishermen,
for James and John –
they came with me
and the dance went on.

3. I danced on the Sabbath
and I cured the lame;
the holy people,
they said it was a shame.
They whipped and they stripped
and they hung me on high,
and they left me there
on a cross to die.

4. I danced on a Friday
when the sky turned black –
it's hard to dance
with the devil on your back.
They buried my body,
and they thought I'd gone,
but I am the dance,
and I still go on.

5. They cut me down
and I leapt up high;
I am the life
that'll never, never die;
I'll live in you
if you'll live in me –
I am the Lord
of the Dance, said he.

108

Horatius Bonar (1808-1889)

1. I heard the voice of Jesus say,
'Come unto me and rest;
lay down, thou weary one, lay down
thy head upon my breast.'
I came to Jesus as I was,
so weary, worn and sad;
I found in him a resting-place,
and he has made me glad.

2. I heard the voice of Jesus say,
'Behold, I freely give
the living water, thirsty one;
stoop down and drink and live.'
I came to Jesus, and I drank
of that life-giving stream;
my thirst was quenched, my soul revived,
and now I live in him.

3. I heard the voice of Jesus say,
'I am this dark world's light;
look unto me, thy morn shall rise,
and all thy day be bright.'
I looked to Jesus, and I found
in him my star, my sun;
and in that light of life I'll walk
till trav'lling days are done.

109
Walter Chalmers Smith (1824-1908)
based on 1 Timothy 1:17

1. Immortal, invisible,
   God only wise,
   in light inaccessible hid
   from our eyes,
   most blessed, most glorious,
   the Ancient of Days,
   almighty, victorious,
   thy great name we praise.

2. Unresting, unhasting,
   and silent as light,
   nor wanting, nor wasting,
   thou rulest in might;
   thy justice like mountains
   high soaring above
   thy clouds which are fountains
   of goodness and love.

3. To all life thou givest,
   to both great and small;
   in all life thou livest,
   the true life of all;
   we blossom and flourish
   as leaves on the tree,
   and wither and perish;
   but naught changeth thee.

4. Great Father of glory,
   pure Father of light,
   thine angels adore thee,
   all veiling their sight;
   all laud we would render,
   O help us to see
   'tis only the splendour
   of light hideth thee.

110
John Greenleaf Whittier (1807-1892)

1. Immortal love, for ever full,
   for ever flowing free,
   for ever shared, for ever whole,
   a never-ebbing sea.

2. Our outward lips confess the name
   all other names above;
   love only knoweth whence it came
   and comprehendeth love.

3. O warm, sweet, tender, even yet
   a present help is he;
   and faith has still its Olivet,
   and love its Galilee.

4. The healing of his seamless dress
   is by our beds of pain;
   we touch him in life's throng and press,
   and we are whole again.

5. Through him the first fond prayers are said
   our lips of childhood frame;
   the last low whispers of our dead
   are burdened with his name.

6. Alone, O love ineffable,
   thy saving name is giv'n;
   to turn aside from thee is hell,
   to walk with thee is heav'n.

111
Anna Laetitia Waring (1820-1910) based on Psalm 23

1. In heav'nly love abiding,
   no change my heart shall fear;
   and safe is such confiding,
   for nothing changes here.
   The storm may roar without me,
   my heart may low be laid,
   but God is round about me,
   and can I be dismayed?

2. Wherever he may guide me,
   no want shall turn me back;
   my Shepherd is beside me,
   and nothing can I lack.
   His wisdom ever waketh,
   his sight is never dim,
   he knows the way he taketh,
   and I will walk with him.

Continued overleaf

3. Green pastures are before me,
   which yet I have not seen;
   bright skies will soon be o'er me,
   where the dark clouds have been.
   My hope I cannot measure,
   my path to life is free,
   my Saviour has my treasure,
   and he will walk with me.

5. What can I give him,
   poor as I am?
   If I were a shepherd
   I would bring a lamb;
   if I were a wise man
   I would do my part,
   yet what I can I give him:
   give my heart.

112 Christina Georgina Rossetti (1830-1894)

1. In the bleak mid-winter
   frosty wind made moan,
   earth stood hard as iron,
   water like a stone;
   snow had fallen, snow on snow,
   snow on snow,
   in the bleak mid-winter, long ago.

2. Our God, heav'n cannot hold him
   nor earth sustain;
   heav'n and earth shall flee away
   when he comes to reign.
   In the bleak mid-winter
   a stable place sufficed
   the Lord God almighty, Jesus Christ.

3. Enough for him, whom cherubim
   worship night and day,
   a breastful of milk,
   and a mangerful of hay:
   enough for him, whom angels
   fall down before,
   the ox and ass and camel which adore.

4. Angels and archangels
   may have gathered there,
   cherubim and seraphim
   thronged the air;
   but only his mother
   in her maiden bliss
   worshipped the beloved with a kiss.

113 Edmund Hamilton Sears (1810-1876), alt.

1. It came upon the midnight clear,
   that glorious song of old,
   from angels bending near the earth
   to touch their harps of gold:
   'Peace on the earth, goodwill to all,
   from heav'ns' all gracious King!'
   The world in solemn stillness lay
   to hear the angels sing.

2. Still through the cloven skies they come,
   with peaceful wings unfurled;
   and still their heav'nly music floats
   o'er all the weary world:
   above its sad and lowly plains
   they bend on hov'ring wing;
   and ever o'er its Babel-sounds
   the blessèd angels sing.

3. Yet with the woes of sin and strife
   the world has suffered long;
   beneath the angel-strain have rolled
   two thousand years of wrong;
   and warring humankind hears not
   the love-song which they bring;
   O hush the noise of mortal strife,
   and hear the angels sing!

4. And ye, beneath life's crushing load,
   whose forms are bending low,
   who toil along the climbing way
   with painful steps and slow:
   look now! for glad and golden hours
   come swiftly on the wing;
   O rest beside the weary road,
   and hear the angels sing.

5. For lo, the days are hast'ning on,
   by prophets seen of old,
   when with the ever-circling years
   comes round the age of gold;
   when peace shall over all the earth
   its ancient splendours fling,
   and all the world give back the song
   which now the angels sing.

114 Dan Schutte, based on Isaiah 6
© 1981 Daniel L. Schutte and New Dawn Music

1. I, the Lord of sea and sky,
   I have heard my people cry.
   All who dwell in dark and sin
   my hand will save.
   I who made the stars of night,
   I will make their darkness bright.
   Who will bear my light to them?
   Whom shall I send?

   Here I am, Lord. Is it I, Lord?
   I have heard you calling in the night.
   I will go, Lord, if you lead me.
   I will hold your people in my heart.

2. I, the Lord of snow and rain,
   I have borne my people's pain.
   I have wept for love of them.
   They turn away.
   I will break their hearts of stone,
   give them hearts for love alone.
   I will speak my word to them.
   Whom shall I send?

3. I, the Lord of wind and flame,
   I will tend the poor and lame.
   I will set a feast for them.
   My hand will save.
   Finest bread I will provide
   till their hearts be satisfied.
   I will give my life to them.
   Whom shall I send?

115 William Walsham How (1823-1897)

1. It is a thing most wonderful,
   almost too wonderful to be,
   that God's own Son should come from
     heav'n,
   and die to save a child like me.

2. And yet I know that it is true:
   he chose a poor and humble lot,
   and wept and toiled, and mourned and
     died,
   for love of those who loved him not.

3. I cannot tell how he could love
   a child so weak and full of sin;
   his love must be most wonderful,
   if he could die my love to win.

4. I sometimes think about the cross,
   and shut my eyes, and try to see
   the cruel nails and crown of thorns,
   and Jesus crucified for me.

5. But even could I see him die,
   I could but see a little part
   of that great love which, like a fire,
   is always burning in his heart.

6. It is most wonderful to know
   his love for me so free and sure;
   but 'tis more wonderful to see
   my love for him so faint and poor.

7. And yet I want to love thee, Lord;
   O light the flame within my heart,
   and I will love thee more and more,
   until I see thee as thou art.

116 Leona von Brethorst
© 1976 Maranatha! Music/CopyCare

I will enter his gates
with thanksgiving in my heart,
I will enter his courts with praise,
I will say this is the day
that the Lord has made,
I will rejoice for he has made me glad.
He has made me glad, he has made me glad,
I will rejoice for he has made me glad.
He has made me glad, he had made me glad,
I will rejoice for he has made me glad.

117 'De Contemptu Mundi' by St. Bernard of Cluny,
12th century, trans. John Mason Neale (1818-1866), alt.

1. Jerusalem the golden,
   with milk and honey blest,
   beneath thy contemplation
   sink heart and voice oppressed.
   I know not, ah, I know not
   what joys await us there,
   what radiancy of glory,
   what bliss beyond compare.

2. They stand, those halls of Zion,
   all jubilant with song,
   and bright with many angels,
   and all the martyr throng;
   the prince is ever with them,
   the daylight is serene;
   the pastures of the blessèd
   are decked in glorious sheen.

3. There is the throne of David;
   and there, from care released,
   the shout of them that triumph,
   the song of them that feast;
   and they, who with their leader
   have fully run the race,
   are robed in white for ever
   before their Saviour's face.

4. O sweet and blessèd country,
   the home of God's elect!
   O sweet and blessèd country,
   that eager hearts expect!
   Jesus, in mercy, bring us
   to that dear land of rest;
   who art, with God the Father
   and Spirit, ever blest.

118 Charles Wesley (1707-1788) alt.

1. Jesu, lover of my soul,
   let me to thy bosom fly,
   while the gath'ring waters roll,
   while the tempest still is high:
   hide me, O my Saviour, hide,
   till the storm of life is past;
   safe into the haven guide,
   O receive my soul at last.

2. Other refuge have I none,
   hangs my helpless soul on thee;
   leave, ah, leave me not alone,
   still support and comfort me.
   All my trust on thee is stayed,
   all my help from thee I bring;
   cover my defenceless head
   with the shadow of thy wing.

3. Plenteous grace with thee is found,
   grace to cleanse from ev'ry sin;
   let the healing streams abound,
   make and keep me pure within.
   Thou of life the fountain art,
   freely let me take of thee,
   spring thou up within my heart,
   rise to all eternity.

119 Cecil Frances Alexander (1818-1895)

1. Jesus calls us: o'er the tumult
   of our life's wild, restless sea;
   day by day his sweet voice soundeth,
   saying, 'Christian, follow me.'

2. As of old Saint Andrew heard it
by the Galilean lake,
turned from home and toil and kindred,
leaving all for his dear sake.

3. Jesus calls us from the worship
of the vain world's golden store,
from each idol that would keep us,
saying, 'Christian, love me more.'

4. In our joys and in our sorrows,
days of toil and hours of ease,
still he calls, in cares and pleasures,
that we love him more than these.

5. Jesus call us: by thy mercies,
Saviour, make us hear thy call,
give our hearts to thine obedience,
serve and love thee best of all.

120 Matt Redman
© 1995 Thankyou Music

1. Jesus Christ, I think upon your sacrifice;
you became nothing, poured out to death.
Many times I've wondered at your gift
of life,
and I'm in that place once again,
I'm in that place once again.

And once again I look upon
the cross where you died.
I'm humbled by your mercy
and I'm broken inside.
Once again I thank you,
once again I pour out my life.

2. Now you are exalted to the highest place,
King of the heavens, where one day
I'll bow.
But for now I marvel at this saving grace,
and I'm full of praise once again,
I'm full of praise once again.

Thank you for the cross, thank you for
the cross,
thank you for the cross, my friend.
Thank you for the cross, thank you for
the cross,
thank you for the cross, my friend.

121 v.1: 'Surrexit hodie (14th Century) trans. anon.
as in 'Lyra Davidica' (1708) vs. 2-3 from J. Arnold's
Compleat Psalmodist (1749)

1. Jesus Christ is ris'n today, alleluia!
our triumphant holy day, alleluia!
who did once, upon the cross, alleluia!
suffer to redeem our loss, alleluia!

2. Hymns of praise then let us sing, alleluia!
unto Christ, our heav'nly King, alleluia!
who endured the cross and grave, alleluia!
sinners to redeem and save, alleluia!

3. But the pains that he endured, alleluia!
our salvation have procured; alleluia!
now above the sky he's King, alleluia!
where the angels ever sing, alleluia!

122 Percy Dearmer (1867-1936)
after John Mason Neale (1818-1866) alt.
© Oxford University Press

1. Jesus, good above all other,
gentle child of gentle mother,
in a stable born our brother,
give us grace to persevere.

2. Jesus, cradled in a manger,
for us facing ev'ry danger,
living as a homeless stranger,
make we thee our King most dear.

3. Jesus, for thy people dying,
risen Master, death defying,
Lord in heav'n thy grace supplying,
keep us to thy presence near.

4. Jesus, who our sorrows bearest,
all our thoughts and hopes thou sharest,
thou to us the truth declarest;
help us all thy truth to hear.

5. Lord, in all our doings guide us;
pride and hate shall ne'er divide us;
we'll go on with thee beside us,
and with joy we'll persevere.

123

David J. Mansell
© 1982 Word's Spirit of Praise Music
Administered by CopyCare

1. Jesus is Lord!
   Creation's voice proclaims it,
   for by his pow'r each tree and flow'r
   was planned and made.
   Jesus is Lord! The universe declares it;
   sun, moon and stars in heaven cry:
   Jesus is Lord!

   Jesus is Lord! Jesus is Lord!
   Praise him with alleluias
   for Jesus is Lord!

2. Jesus is Lord!
   Yet from his throne eternal
   in flesh he came to die in pain
   on Calv'ry's tree.
   Jesus is Lord! From him all life proceeding,
   yet gave his life as ransom
   thus setting us free.

3. Jesus is Lord!
   O'er sin the mighty conqu'ror,
   from death he rose and all his foes
   shall own his name.
   Jesus is Lord! God sends his Holy Spirit
   to show by works of power
   that Jesus is Lord.

124

Christian Fürchtegott Gellert (1715-1769)
trans. Frances Elizabeth Cox (1812-1897) alt.

1. Jesus lives! thy terrors now
   can no more, O death, appal us;
   Jesus lives! by this we know
   thou, O grave, canst not enthral us.
   Alleluia.

2. Jesus lives! henceforth is death
   but the gate of life immortal:
   this shall calm our trembling breath,
   when we pass its gloomy portal.
   Alleluia.

3. Jesus lives! for us he died;
   then, alone to Jesus living,
   pure in heart may we abide,
   glory to our Saviour giving.
   Alleluia.

4. Jesus lives! our hearts know well
   naught from us his love shall sever;
   life nor death nor pow'rs of hell
   tear us from his keeping ever.
   Alleluia.

5. Jesus lives! to him the throne
   over all the world is given:
   may we go where he is gone,
   rest and reign with him in heaven.
   Alleluia.

125

Isaac Watts (1674-1748)

1. Jesus shall reign where'er the sun
   does his successive journeys run;
   his kingdom stretch from shore to shore,
   till moons shall wax and wane no more.

2. People and realms of ev'ry tongue
   dwell on his love with sweetest song,
   and infant voices shall proclaim
   their early blessings on his name.

3. Blessings abound where'er he reigns:
   the pris'ners leap to lose their chains;
   the weary find eternal rest,
   and all the humble poor are blest.

4. To him shall endless prayer be made,
   and praises throng to crown his head;
   his name like incense shall arise
   with ev'ry morning sacrifice.

5. Let ev'ry creature rise and bring
   peculiar honours to our King;
   angels descend with songs again,
   and earth repeat the loud amen.

126

St Bernard of Clairvaux (1091-1153)
trans. Edward Caswall (1814-1878) alt.

1. Jesu, the very thought of thee
   with sweetness fills the breast;
   but sweeter far thy face to see,
   and in thy presence rest.

2. No voice can sing, no heart can frame,
   nor can the mem'ry find,
   a sweeter sound than Jesu's name,
   the Saviour of mankind.

3. O hope of ev'ry contrite heart,
   O joy of all the meek,
   to those who ask how kind thou art,
   how good to those who seek!

4. But what to those who find? Ah, this
   nor tongue nor pen can show;
   the love of Jesus, what it is
   his true disciples know.

5. Jesu, our only joy be thou,
   as thou our prize wilt be;
   in thee be all our glory now,
   and through eternity.

127

Fred Dunn (1907-1979)
© 1977 Thankyou Music

Jubilate, ev'rybody,
serve the Lord in all your ways and
come before his presence singing;
enter now his courts with praise.
For the Lord our God is gracious,
and his mercy everlasting.
Jubilate, jubilate, jubilate, Deo!

128

Charlotte Elliott (1789-1871)

1. Just as I am, without one plea
   but that thy blood was shed for me,
   and that thou bidst me come to thee,
   O Lamb of God, I come.

2. Just as I am, though tossed about
   with many a conflict, many a doubt,
   fightings and fears within, without,
   O Lamb of God, I come.

3. Just as I am, poor, wretched, blind;
   sight, riches, healing of the mind,
   yea, all I need, in thee to find,
   O Lamb of God, I come.

4. Just as I am, thou wilt receive,
   wilt welcome, pardon, cleanse, relieve:
   because thy promise I believe,
   O Lamb of God, I come.

5. Just as I am, thy love unknown
   has broken ev'ry barrier down,
   now to be thine, yea, thine alone,
   O Lamb of God, I come.

6. Just as I am, of that free love
   the breadth, length, depth and height
       to prove,
   here for a season, then above,
   O Lamb of God, I come.

129

George Herbert (1593-1633)

1. King of glory, King of peace,
   I will love thee;
   and, that love may never cease,
   I will move thee.
   Thou hast granted my appeal,
   thou hast heard me;
   thou didst note my ardent zeal,
   thou hast spared me.

2. Wherefore with my utmost art,
   I will sing thee,
   and the cream of all my heart
   I will bring thee.
   Though my sins against me cried,
   thou didst clear me,
   and alone, when they replied,
   thou didst hear me.

Continued overleaf

3. Sev'n whole days, not one in sev'n,
   I will praise thee;
   in my heart, though not in heav'n,
   I can raise thee.
   Small it is, in this poor sort
   to enrol thee:
   e'en eternity's too short
   to extol thee.

130 John Henry Newman (1801-1890)

1. Lead, kindly light,
   amid th'encircling gloom,
   lead thou me on;
   the night is dark,
   and I am far from home;
   lead thou me on.
   Keep thou my feet;
   I do not ask to see
   the distant scene;
   one step enough for me.

2. I was not ever thus,
   nor prayed that thou
   shouldst lead me on;
   I loved to choose
   and see my path; but now
   lead thou me on.
   I loved the garish day,
   and, spite of fears,
   pride ruled my will:
   remember not past years.

3. So long thy pow'r
   hath blest me, sure it still
   will lead me on,
   o'er moor and fen,
   o'er crag and torrent, till
   the night is gone;
   and with the morn
   those angel faces smile,
   which I have loved long since,
   and lost awhile.

131 James Edmeston (1791-1867)

1. Lead us, heav'nly Father, lead us
   o'er the world's tempestuous sea;
   guard us, guide us, keep us, feed us,
   for we have no help but thee;
   yet possessing ev'ry blessing
   if our God our Father be.

2. Saviour, breathe forgiveness o'er us,
   all our weakness thou dost know,
   thou didst tread this earth before us,
   thou didst feel its keenest woe;
   lone and dreary, faint and weary,
   through the desert thou didst go.

3. Spirit of our God, descending,
   fill our hearts with heav'nly joy,
   love with ev'ry passion blending,
   pleasure that can never cloy;
   thus provided, pardoned, guided,
   nothing can our peace destroy.

132 George Herbert (1593-1633)

1. Let all the world in ev'ry corner sing,
   my God and King!
   The heav'ns are not too high,
   his praise may thither fly;
   the earth is not too low,
   his praises there may grow.
   Let all the world in ev'ry corner sing,
   my God and King!

2. Let all the world in ev'ry corner sing,
   my God and King!
   The Church with psalms must shout,
   no door can keep them out;
   but, above all, the heart
   must bear the longest part.
   Let all the world in ev'ry corner sing,
   my God and King!

133

John Milton (1608-1674), based on Psalm 136

1. Let us, with a gladsome mind,
   praise the Lord, for he is kind;

   for his mercies ay endure,
   ever faithful, ever sure.

2. Let us blaze his name abroad,
   for of gods he is the God;

3, He, with all-commanding might,
   filled the new-made world with light;

4. He the golden-tressèd sun
   caused all day his course to run;

5. And the moon to shine at night,
   'mid her starry sisters bright;

6. All things living he doth feed,
   his full hand supplies their need;

7. Let us, with a gladsome mind,
   praise the Lord, for he is kind;

134

George William Kitchin (1827-1912) and
Michael Robert Newbolt (1874-1956), alt.
© Hymns Ancient & Modern Ltd.

Lift high the Cross,
the love of Christ proclaim
till all the world adore his sacred name!

1. Come, Christians,
   follow where our Saviour trod,
   o'er death victorious,
   Christ the Son of God.

2. Led on their way by this
   triumphant sign,
   the hosts of God in joyful
   praise combine:

3. Each new disciple
   of the Crucified
   is called to bear the seal
   of him who died:

4. Saved by the Cross
   whereon their Lord was slain,
   now Adam's children
   their lost home regain:

5. From north and south,
   from east and west they raise
   in growing harmony
   their song of praise:

6. O Lord, once lifted
   on the glorious tree,
   as thou hast promised,
   draw us unto thee:

7. Let ev'ry race
   and ev'ry language tell
   of him who saves
   from fear of death and hell:

8. From farthest regions,
   let them homage bring,
   and on his Cross
   adore their Saviour King:

9. Set up thy throne,
   that earth's despair may cease
   beneath the shadow
   of its healing peace:

10. For thy blest Cross
    which doth for all atone,
    creation's praises rise
    before thy throne:

11. So let the world
    proclaim with one accord
    the praise of our
    ever-living Lord.

135

Ascribed to Thomas à Kempis (c. 1379-1471)
trans. John Mason Neale (1818-1866)

1. Light's abode, celestial Salem,
   vision whence true peace doth spring,
   brighter than the heart can fancy,
   mansion of the highest King;
   O how glorious are the praises
   which of thee the prophets sing!

Continued overleaf

2. There for ever and for ever
   alleluia is outpoured;
   for unending, for unbroken
   is the feast-day of the Lord;
   all is pure and all is holy
   that within thy walls is stored.

3. There no cloud or passing vapour
   dims the brightness of the air;
   endless noon-day, glorious noon-day,
   from the Sun of suns is there;
   there no night brings rest from labour,
   for unknown are toil and care.

4. O how glorious and resplendent,
   fragile body, shalt thou be,
   when endued with so much beauty,
   full of health and strong and free,
   full of vigour, full of pleasure
   that shall last eternally.

5. Now with gladness, now with courage,
   bear the burden on thee laid,
   that hereafter these thy labours
   may with endless gifts be paid;
   and in everlasting glory
   thou with brightness be arrayed.

6. Laud and honour to the Father,
   laud and honour to the Son,
   laud and honour to the Spirit,
   ever Three and ever One,
   consubstantial, co-eternal,
   while unending ages run.

136 Charles Wesley (1707-1788), John Cennick (1718-1755) and Martin Madan (1728-1790)

1. Lo, he comes with clouds descending,
   once for mortal sinners slain;
   thousand thousand saints attending
   swell the triumph of his train.
   Alleluia! Alleluia! Alleluia!
   Christ appears on earth to reign.

2. Ev'ry eye shall now behold him
   robed in dreadful majesty;
   we who set at naught and sold him,
   pierced and nailed him to the tree,
   deeply grieving, deeply grieving,
      deeply grieving,
   shall the true Messiah see.

3. Those dear tokens of his passion
   still his dazzling body bears,
   cause of endless exultation
   to his ransomed worshippers:
   with what rapture, with what rapture,
      with what rapture
   gaze we on those glorious scars!

4. Yea, amen, let all adore thee,
   high on thine eternal throne;
   Saviour, take the pow'r and glory,
   claim the kingdom for thine own.
   Alleluia! Alleluia! Alleluia!
   Thou shalt reign, and thou alone.

137 Timothy Dudley-Smith (b. 1926)
© *Timothy Dudley-Smith*

1. Lord, for the years
   your love has kept and guided,
   urged and inspired us,
   cheered us on our way,
   sought us and saved us,
   pardoned and provided:
   Lord of the years,
   we bring our thanks today.

2. Lord, for that word,
   the word of life which fires us,
   speaks to our hearts
   and sets our souls ablaze,
   teaches and trains,
   rebukes us and inspires us:
   Lord of the word,
   receive your people's praise.

3. Lord, for our land
   in this our generation,
   spirits oppressed by pleasure,
   wealth and care:
   for young and old,
   for commonwealth and nation,
   Lord of our land,
   be pleased to hear our prayer.

4. Lord, for our world;
   when we disown and doubt him,
   loveless in strength,
   and comfortless in pain,
   hungry and helpless,
   lost indeed without him,
   Lord of the world,
   we pray that Christ may reign.

5. Lord, for ourselves;
   in living power remake us,
   self on the cross
   and Christ upon the throne;
   past put behind us,
   for the future take us,
   Lord of our lives,
   to live for Christ alone.

138 Patrick Appleford (b. 1925)
© 1960 Josef Weinberger Ltd.

1. Lord Jesus Christ, you have come to us,
   you are one with us, Mary's Son.
   Cleansing our souls from all their sin,
   pouring your love and goodness in,
   Jesus, our love for you we sing,
   living Lord.

2. Lord Jesus Christ, now and ev'ry day
   teach us how to pray, Son of God.
   You have commanded us to do
   this in remembrance, Lord, of you.
   Into our lives your pow'r breaks through,
   living Lord.

3. Lord Jesus Christ, you have come to us,
   born as one of us, Mary's Son.
   Led out to die on Calvary,
   risen from death to set us free,
   living Lord Jesus, help us see
   you are Lord.

4. Lord Jesus Christ, I would come to you,
   live my life for you, Son of God.
   All your commands I know are true,
   your many gifts will make me new,
   into my life your pow'r breaks through,
   living Lord.

139 Bishop Synesius (375-430)
trans. Allen William Chatfield (1808-1896)

1. Lord Jesus, think on me,
   and purge away my sin;
   from earth-born passions set me free,
   and make me pure within.

2. Lord Jesus, think on me,
   with care and woe opprest;
   let me thy loving servant be
   and taste thy promised rest.

3. Lord Jesus, think on me
   amid the battle's strife;
   in all my pain and misery
   be thou my health and life.

4. Lord Jesus, think on me,
   nor let me go astray;
   through darkness and perplexity
   point thou the heav'nly way.

5. Lord Jesus, think on me,
   when flows the tempest high:
   when on doth rush the enemy,
   O Saviour, be thou nigh.

6. Lord Jesus, think on me,
   that, when the flood is past,
   I may th'eternal brightness see,
   and share thy joy at last.

140

Jan Struther (1901-1953)
© Oxford University Press

1. Lord of all hopefulness,
   Lord of all joy,
   whose trust, ever childlike,
   no cares could destroy,
   be there at our waking,
   and give us, we pray,
   your bliss in our hearts, Lord,
   at the break of the day.

2. Lord of all eagerness,
   Lord of all faith,
   whose strong hands were skilled
   at the plane and the lathe,
   be there at our labours,
   and give us, we pray,
   your strength in our hearts, Lord,
   at the noon of the day.

3. Lord of all kindliness,
   Lord of all grace,
   your hands swift to welcome,
   your arms to embrace,
   be there at our homing,
   and give us, we pray,
   your love in our hearts, Lord,
   at the eve of the day.

4. Lord of all gentleness,
   Lord of all calm,
   whose voice is contentment,
   whose presence is balm,
   be there at our sleeping,
   and give us, we pray,
   your peace in our hearts, Lord,
   at the end of the day.

141

Graham Kendrick (b. 1950)
© 1987 Make Way Music

1. Lord, the light of your love is shining,
   in the midst of the darkness, shining;
   Jesus, Light of the World, shine upon us,
   set us free by the truth you now bring us.
   Shine on me, shine on me.

Shine, Jesus, shine,
fill this land with the Father's glory;
blaze, Spirit, blaze,
set our hearts on fire.
Flow, river, flow,
flood the nations with grace and mercy;
send forth your word, Lord,
and let there be light.

2. Lord, I come to your awesome presence,
   from the shadows into your radiance;
   by the blood I may enter your brightness,
   search me, try me, consume all
       my darkness.
   Shine on me, shine on me.

3. As we gaze on your kingly brightness,
   so our faces display your likeness,
   ever changing from glory to glory;
   mirrored here may our lives tell your story.
   Shine on me, shine on me.

142

Henry Williams Baker (1821-1877)

1. Lord, thy word abideth,
   and our footsteps guideth;
   who its truth believeth
   light and joy receiveth.

2. When our foes are near us,
   then thy word doth cheer us,
   word of consolation,
   message of salvation.

3. When the storms are o'er us,
   and dark clouds before us,
   then its light directeth,
   and our way protecteth.

4. Who can tell the pleasure,
   who recount the treasure,
   by thy word imparted
   to the simple-hearted?

5. Word of mercy, giving
   succour to the living;
   word of life, supplying
   comfort to the dying.

6. O that we, discerning
   its most holy learning,
   Lord, may love and fear thee,
   evermore be near thee.

143 Charles Wesley (1707-1788)

1. Love divine, all loves excelling,
   joy of heav'n, to earth come down,
   fix in us thy humble dwelling,
   all thy faithful mercies crown.

2. Jesu, thou art all compassion,
   pure unbounded love thou art;
   visit us with thy salvation,
   enter ev'ry trembling heart.

3. Breathe, O breathe thy loving Spirit
   into ev'ry troubled breast;
   let us all in thee inherit,
   let us find thy promised rest.

4. Take away the love of sinning,
   Alpha and Omega be;
   end of faith, as its beginning,
   set our hearts at liberty.

5. Come, almighty to deliver,
   let us all thy grace receive;
   suddenly return, and never,
   never more thy temples leave.

6. Thee we would be always blessing,
   serve thee as thy hosts above;
   pray, and praise thee without ceasing,
   glory in thy perfect love.

7. Finish then thy new creation,
   pure and spotless let us be;
   let us see thy great salvation
   perfectly restored in thee.

8. Changed from glory into glory,
   till in heav'n we take our place,
   till we cast our crowns before thee,
   lost in wonder, love, and praise.

144 Charles Wesley (1707-1788)

1. Love's redeeming work is done;
   fought the fight, the battle won:
   lo, our Sun's eclipse is o'er,
   lo, he sets in blood no more.

2. Vain the stone, the watch, the seal;
   Christ has burst the gates of hell;
   death in vain forbids his rise;
   Christ has opened paradise.

3. Lives again our glorious King;
   where, O death, is now thy sting?
   Dying once, he all doth save;
   where thy victory, O grave?

4. Soar we now where Christ has led,
   foll'wing our exalted Head;
   made like him, like him we rise;
   ours the cross, the grave, the skies.

5. Hail the Lord of earth and heav'n!
   praise to thee by both be giv'n;
   thee we greet triumphant now;
   hail, the Resurrection thou!

145 Jane Elizabeth Leeson (1809-1881)

1. Loving Shepherd of thy sheep,
   keep me, Lord, in safety keep;
   nothing can thy pow'r withstand,
   none can pluck me from thy hand.

2. Loving Shepherd, thou didst give
   thine own life that I might live;
   may I love thee day by day,
   gladly thy sweet will obey.

3. Loving Shepherd, ever near,
   teach me still thy voice to hear;
   suffer not my steps to stray
   from the straight and narrow way.

4. Where thou leadest may I go,
   walking in thy steps below;
   then, before thy Father's throne,
   Jesu, claim me for thine own.

146 Jack W. Hayford (b. 1934)

Majesty, worship his majesty;
unto Jesus be glory, honour and praise.
Majesty, kingdom authority
flow from his throne unto his own:
his anthem raise.
So exalt, lift up on high the name of Jesus;
magnify, come glorify Christ Jesus the King.
Majesty, worship his majesty,
Jesus who died, now glorified,
King of all kings.

147 Sebastian Temple (1928-1997)
based on the Prayer of St Francis

1. Make me a channel of your peace.
   Where there is hatred, let me bring
       your love.
   Where there is injury, your pardon, Lord;
   and where there's doubt, true faith in you.

   O, Master, grant that I may never seek
   so much to be consoled as to console,
   to be understood as to understand,
   to be loved as to love with all my soul.

2. Make me a channel of your peace.
   Where there's despair in life, let me
       bring hope.
   Where there is darkness, only light,
   and where there's sadness, ever joy.

3. Make me a channel of your peace.
   It is in pardoning that we are pardoned,
   in giving of ourselves that we receive,
   and in dying that we're born to eternal life.

148 Graham Kendrick (b. 1950)

1. Make way, make way, for Christ the King
   in splendour arrives;
   fling wide the gates and welcome him
   into your lives.

   Make way (make way), make way (make way),
   for the King of kings (for the King of kings);
   make way (make way), make way (make way),
   and let his kingdom in!

2. He comes the broken hearts to heal,
   the pris'ners to free;
   the deaf shall hear, the lame shall dance,
   the blind shall see.

3. And those who mourn with heavy hearts,
   who weep and sigh,
   with laughter, joy and royal crown
   he'll beautify.

4. We call you now to worship him
   as Lord of all,
   to have no gods before him,
   their thrones must fall.

149 Graham Kendrick (b. 1950)

1. Meekness and majesty,
   manhood and deity,
   in perfect harmony, the Man who is God.
   Lord of eternity dwells in humanity,
   kneels in humility and washes our feet.

   O what a mystery, meekness and majesty.
   Bow down and worship for this is your God,
   this is your God.

2. Father's pure radiance,
   perfect in innocence,
   yet learns obedience to death on a cross.
   Suff'ring to give us life,
       conqu'ring through sacrifice,
   and as they crucify prays: 'Father forgive.'

3. Wisdom unsearchable,
   God the invisible,
   love indestructible in frailty appears.
   Lord of infinity, stooping so tenderly,
   lifts our humanity to the heights of
       his throne.

150 Eleanor Farjeon (1881-1965)
© David Higham Associates.

1. Morning has broken like the first morning,
   blackbird has spoken like the first bird.
   Praise for the singing!
     Praise for the morning!
   Praise for them, springing
     fresh from the Word!

2. Sweet the rain's new fall, sunlit from heaven,
   like the first dew-fall on the first grass.
   Praise for the sweetness of the wet garden,
   sprung in completeness where his feet pass.

3. Mine is the sunlight! Mine is the morning
   born of the one light Eden saw play!
   Praise with elation, praise ev'ry morning,
   God's re-creation of the new day!

151 Philip Doddridge (1702-1751), alt.
v 3 Michael Forster (b. 1946)
© 1996 Kevin Mayhew Ltd.

1. My God, and is thy table spread,
   and does thy cup with love o'erflow?
   Thither be all thy children led,
   and let them all thy sweetness know.

2. Hail, sacred feast, which Jesus makes!
   Rich banquet of his flesh and blood!
   Thrice happy all, who here partake
   that sacred stream, that heav'nly food.

3. What wondrous love! What perfect grace,
   for Jesus, our exalted host,
   invites us to this special place
   who offer least and need the most.

4. O let thy table honoured be,
   and furnished well with joyful guests;
   and may each soul salvation see,
   that here its sacred pledges tastes.

152 Latin (17th century)
trans. Edward Caswall (1814-1878)

1. My God, I love thee; not because
   I hope for heav'n thereby,
   nor yet because who love thee not
   are lost eternally.

2. Thou, O my Jesus, thou didst me
   upon the cross embrace;
   for me didst bear the nails and spear,
   and manifold disgrace.

3. And griefs and torments numberless,
   and sweat of agony;
   yea, death itself – and all for me
   who was thine enemy.

4. Then why, O blessèd Jesu Christ,
   should I not love thee well?
   Not for the sake of winning heav'n,
   nor of escaping hell.

5. Not from the hope of gaining aught,
   not seeking a reward;
   but as thyself hast lovèd me,
   O ever-loving Lord.

6. So would I love thee, dearest Lord,
   and in thy praise will sing;
   solely because thou art my God,
   and my most loving King.

153 Darlene Zschech
*© 1993 Darlene Zschech /Hillsong Publishing/
Kingsway Music*

My Jesus, my Saviour,
Lord, there is none like you.
All of my days I want to praise
the wonders of your mighty love.
My comfort, my shelter,
tower of refuge and strength,
let ev'ry breath, all that I am,
never cease to worship you.

Continued overleaf

Shout to the Lord,
all the earth, let us sing
power and majesty,
praise to the King.
Mountains bow down
and the seas will roar
at the sound of your name.
I sing for joy
at the work of your hands.
Forever I'll love you,
forever I'll stand.
Nothing compares to the promise
I have in you.

154 Samuel Crossman (c. 1624-1684) alt.

1. My song is love unknown,
   my Saviour's love to me,
   love to the loveless shown,
   that they might lovely be.
   O who am I, that for my sake,
   my Lord should take frail flesh and die?

2. He came from his blest throne,
   salvation to bestow;
   but men refused, and none
   the longed-for Christ would know.
   But O, my friend, my friend indeed,
   who at my need his life did spend!

3. Sometimes they strew his way,
   and his sweet praises sing:
   resounding all the day
   hosannas to their King:
   then 'Crucify!' is all their breath,
   and for his death they thirst and cry.

4. Why what hath my Lord done?
   What makes this rage and spite?
   He made the lame to run,
   he gave the blind their sight.
   Sweet injuries! Yet they at these
   themselves displease,
      and 'gainst him rise.

5. They rise, and needs will have
   my dear Lord made away;
   a murderer they save,
   the Prince of Life they slay.
   Yet cheerful he to suff'ring goes,
   that he his foes from thence might free.

6. Here might I stay and sing,
   no story so divine;
   never was love, dear King,
   never was grief like thine.
   This is my friend in whose sweet praise
   I all my days could gladly spend.

155 Sarah Flower Adams (1805-1848)

1. Nearer, my God, to thee,
   nearer to thee!
   E'en though it be a cross
   that raiseth me:
   still all my song would be,
   'Nearer, my God, to thee,
   nearer, my God, to thee,
   nearer to thee.'

2. Though, like the wanderer,
   the sun gone down,
   darkness be over me,
   my rest a stone;
   yet in my dreams I'd be
   nearer, my God, to thee,
   nearer, my God, to thee,
   nearer to thee!

3. There let the way appear,
   steps unto heav'n;
   all that thou sendest me
   in mercy giv'n:
   angels to beckon me
   nearer, my God, to thee,
   nearer, my God, to thee,
   nearer to thee!

4. Then, with my waking thoughts
   bright with thy praise,
   out of my stony griefs
   Bethel I'll raise;
   so by my woes to be
   nearer, my God, to thee,
   nearer, my God, to thee,
   nearer to thee!

5. Or if on joyful wing
   cleaving the sky,
   sun, moon and stars forgot,
   upwards I fly,
   still all my song shall be,
   'Nearer, my God, to thee,
   nearer, my God, to thee,
   nearer to thee.'

156 John Keble (1792-1866) based on Lamentations 3:23

1. New ev'ry morning is the love
   our wak'ning and uprising prove;
   through sleep and darkness safely
      brought,
   restored to life and pow'r and thought.

2. New mercies, each returning day,
   hover around us while we pray;
   new perils past, new sins forgiv'n,
   new thoughts of God, new hopes of
      heav'n.

3. If on our daily course our mind
   be set to hallow all we find,
   new treasures still, of countless price,
   God will provide for sacrifice.

4. Old friends, old scenes, will lovelier be,
   as more of heav'n in each we see;
   some soft'ning gleam of love and pray'r
   shall dawn on ev'ry cross and care.

5. The trivial round, the common task,
   will furnish all we need to ask,
   room to deny ourselves, a road
   to bring us daily nearer God.

6. Only, O Lord, in thy dear love
   fit us for perfect rest above;
   and help us, this and ev'ry day,
   to live more nearly as we pray.

157 Martin Rinkart (1586-1649)
trans. Catherine Winkworth (1827-1878)

1. Now thank we all our God,
   with hearts and hands and voices,
   who wondrous things hath done,
   in whom his world rejoices;
   who from our mother's arms
   hath blessed us on our way
   with countless gifts of love,
   and still is ours today.

2. O may this bounteous God
   through all our life be near us,
   with ever joyful hearts
   and blessèd peace to cheer us;
   and keep us in his grace,
   and guide us when perplexed,
   and free us from all ills
   in this world and the next.

3. All praise and thanks to God
   the Father now be given,
   the Son and him who reigns
   with them in highest heaven,
   the one eternal God,
   whom earth and heav'n adore;
   for thus it was, is now,
   and shall be evermore.

158 John Macleod Campbell Crum (1872-1958), alt.
© 1928 Oxford University Press

1. Now the green blade riseth
   from the buried grain,
   wheat that in the dark earth
   many days has lain;
   Love lives again,
   that with the dead has been:
   Love is come again,
   like wheat that springeth green.

Continued overleaf

2. In the grave they laid him,
   Love by hatred slain,
   thinking that never
   he would wake again,
   laid in the earth
   like grain that sleeps unseen:
   Love is come again,
   like wheat that springeth green.

3. Forth he came at Easter,
   like the risen grain,
   he that for three days
   in the grave had lain;
   quick from the dead,
   my risen Lord is seen:
   Love is come again,
   like wheat that springeth green.

4. When our hearts are wintry,
   grieving or in pain,
   thy touch can call us
   back to life again;
   fields of our hearts,
   that dead and bare have been:
   Love is come again,
   like wheat that springeth green.

159
Elizabeth Ann Porter Head (1850-1936)
© Copyright control

1. O Breath of Life,
      come sweeping through us,
   revive your Church with life and pow'r;
   O Breath of Life, come cleanse,
      renew us,
   and fit your Church to meet this hour.

2. O Breath of Love,
      come breathe within us,
   renewing thought and will and heart;
   come, love of Christ, afresh to win us,
   revive your Church in ev'ry part!

3. O Wind of God,
      come bend us, break us,
   till humbly we confess our need;
   then, in your tenderness remake us,
   revive, restore – for this we plead.

4. Revive us, Lord; is zeal abating
   while harvest fields are vast and white?
   Revive us, Lord, the world is waiting –
   equip thy Church to spread the light.

160
Attributed to John Francis Wade (1711-1786)
trans. Frederick Oakeley (1802-1880) and others

1. O come, all ye faithful,
   joyful and triumphant,
   O come ye, O come ye to Bethlehem;
   come and behold him,
      born the king of angels:

   O come, let us adore him,
   O come let us adore him,
   O come, let us adore him,
   Christ the Lord.

2. God of God,
   Light of Light,
   lo, he abhors not the Virgin's womb;
   very God, begotten not created:

3. See how the shepherds,
   summoned to his cradle,
   leaving their flocks, draw nigh with lowly
      fear;
   we too will thither bend our joyful
      footsteps:

4. Lo, star-led chieftains,
   Magi, Christ adoring,
   offer him incense, gold and myrrh;
   we to the Christ-child bring our hearts'
      oblations:

5. Child, for us sinners
   poor and in the manger,
   fain we embrace thee, with love and awe;
   who would not love thee, loving us so
      dearly?

6. Sing, choirs of angels,
   sing in exultation,
   sing, all ye citizens of heav'n above;
   glory to God in the highest:

7. Yea, Lord, we greet thee,
   born this happy morning,
   Jesu, to thee be glory giv'n;
   Word of the Father, now in flesh
      appearing:

161 from the 'Great O Antiphons' (12th - 13th century) trans. John Mason Neale (1818-1866)

1. O come, O come, Emmanuel,
   and ransom captive Israel,
   that mourns in lonely exile here,
   until the Son of God appear.

   Rejoice, rejoice!
   Emmanuel shall come to thee,
   O Israel.

2. O come, thou rod of Jesse, free
   thine own from Satan's tyranny;
   from depths of hell thy people save,
   and give them vict'ry o'er the grave.

3. O come, thou dayspring, come and
      cheer
   our spirits by thine advent here;
   disperse the gloomy clouds of night,
   and death's dark shadows put to flight.

4. O come, thou key of David, come
   and open wide our heav'nly home;
   make safe the way that leads on high,
   and close the path to misery.

5. O come, O come, thou Lord of might,
   who to thy tribes on Sinai's height
   in ancient times didst give the Law,
   in cloud and majesty and awe.

162 Henry Ernest Hardy (Father Andrew S.D.C.) (1869-1946) © Copyright Continuum International Book Publishing Ltd

1. O dearest Lord, thy sacred head
   with thorns was pierced for me;
   O pour thy blessing on my head
   that I may think for thee.

2. O dearest Lord, thy sacred hands
   with nails were pierced for me;
   O shed thy blessing on my hands
   that they may work for thee.

3. O dearest Lord, thy sacred feet
   with nails were pierced for me;
   O pour thy blessing on my feet
   that they may follow thee.

4. O dearest Lord, thy sacred heart
   with spear was pierced for me;
   O pour thy Spirit in my heart
   that I may live for thee.

163 William Cowper (1731-1800)

1. O for a closer walk with God,
   a calm and heav'nly frame;
   a light to shine upon the road
   that leads me to the Lamb.

2. What peaceful hours I once enjoyed,
   how sweet their mem'ry still!
   But they have left an aching void
   the world can never fill.

3. The dearest idol I have known,
   whate'er that idol be,
   help me to tear it from thy throne,
   and worship only thee.

4. So shall my walk be close with God,
   calm and serene my frame;
   so purer light shall mark the road
   that leads me to the Lamb.

164 Charles Wesley (1707-1788)

1. O for a thousand tongues to sing
   my dear Redeemer's praise,
   my dear Redeemer's praise,
   the glories of my God and King,
   the triumphs of his grace,
   the triumphs of his grace,
   the triumphs of his grace!

Continued overleaf

2. Jesus! the name that charms our fears,
   that bids our sorrows cease,
   that bids our sorrows cease;
   'tis music in the sinner's ears,
   'tis life and health and peace. (x3)

3. He breaks the pow'r of cancelled sin,
   he sets the pris'ner free,
   he sets the pris'ner free;
   his blood can make the foulest clean;
   his blood availed for me. (x3)

4. He speaks; and, list'ning to his voice,
   new life the dead receive,
   new life the dead receive,
   the mournful broken hearts rejoice,
   the humble poor believe. (x3)

5. Hear him, ye deaf; his praise, ye dumb,
   your loosened tongues employ,
   your loosened tongues employ;
   ye blind, behold your Saviour come;
   and leap, ye lame, for joy! (x3)

6. My gracious Master and my God,
   assist me to proclaim,
   assist me to proclaim
   and spread through all the earth abroad
   the honours of thy name. (x3)

165
Aurelius Clemens Prudentius (348-413)
trans. John Mason Neale (1818-1866), alt.

1. Of the Father's love begotten,
   ere the worlds began to be,
   he is Alpha and Omega,
   he the source, the ending he,
   of the things that are, and have been,
   and that future years shall see,
   evermore and evermore.

2. At his word they were created;
   he commanded; it was done:
   heav'n and earth and depths of ocean
   in their threefold order one;
   all that grows beneath the shining
   of the light of moon and sun,
   evermore and evermore.

3. O that birth for ever blessèd,
   when the Virgin, full of grace,
   by the Holy Ghost conceiving,
   bore the Saviour of our race,
   and the babe, the world's Redeemer,
   first revealed his sacred face,
   evermore and evermore.

4. O ye heights of heav'n, adore him;
   angel hosts, his praises sing;
   pow'rs, dominions, bow before him,
   and extol our God and King:
   let no tongue on earth be silent,
   ev'ry voice in concert ring,
   evermore and evermore.

5. This is he whom seers and sages
   sang of old with one accord;
   whom the writings of the prophets
   promised in their faithful word;
   now he shines, the long-expected;
   let our songs declare his worth,
   evermore and evermore.

6. Christ, to thee, with God the Father,
   and, O Holy Ghost, to thee,
   hymn and chant and high thanksgiving,
   and unwearied praises be;
   honour, glory, and dominion,
   and eternal victory,
   evermore and evermore.

166
Henry Kirke White (1785-1806) and others

1. Oft in danger, oft in woe,
   onward, Christians, onward go;
   bear the toil, endure the strife,
   strengthened with the bread of life.

2. Onward through the desert night,
   keeping faith and vision bright;
   face the challenge of the hour
   trusting in your Saviour's pow'r.

3. Let not sorrow dim your eye,
   soon shall ev'ry tear be dry;
   let not fears your course impede,
   great your strength if great your need.

4. Let your drooping hearts be glad;
   march in faith and honour clad;
   march, nor think the journey long,
   march to hope's eternal song.

5. Onward then, undaunted, move;
   more than faithful God will prove;
   though the raging waters flow,
   Christian pilgrims, onward go.

167 Michael Perry (1942-1996)
© Mrs B. Perry/Jubilate Hymns

1. O God beyond all praising,
   we worship you today,
   and sing the love amazing
   that songs cannot repay;
   for we can only wonder
   at ev'ry gift you send,
   at blessings without number
   and mercies without end:
   we lift our hearts before you
   and wait upon your word,
   we honour and adore you,
   our great and mighty Lord.

2. Then hear, O gracious Saviour,
   accept the love we bring,
   that we who know your favour
   may serve you as our King;
   and whether our tomorrows
   be filled with good or ill,
   we'll triumph through our sorrows
   and rise to bless you still:
   to marvel at your beauty
   and glory in your ways,
   and make a joyful duty
   our sacrifice of praise.

168 Isaac Watts (1674-1748) alt.

1. O God, our help in ages past,
   our hope for years to come,
   our shelter from the stormy blast,
   and our eternal home.

2. Beneath the shadow of thy throne,
   thy saints have dwelt secure;
   sufficient is thine arm alone,
   and our defence is sure.

3. Before the hills in order stood,
   or earth received her frame,
   from everlasting thou art God,
   to endless years the same.

4. A thousand ages in thy sight
   are like an evening gone;
   short as the watch that ends the night
   before the rising sun.

5. Time, like an ever-rolling stream,
   will bear us all away;
   we fade and vanish, as a dream
   dies at the op'ning day.

6. O God, our help in ages past,
   our hope for years to come,
   be thou our guard while troubles last,
   and our eternal home.

169 John Mason Neale (1818-1866) alt
© v6:1996 Kevin Mayhew Ltd.

1. O happy band of pilgrims,
   if onward ye will tread,
   with Jesus as your fellow,
   to Jesus as your head.

2. The cross that Jesus carried
   he carried as your due:
   the crown that Jesus weareth
   he weareth it for you.

3. The faith by which ye see him,
   the hope in which ye yearn,
   the love that through all troubles
   to him alone will turn.

Continued overleaf

4. What are they but forerunners
   to lead you to his sight,
   the longed-for distant dawning
   of uncreated light?

5. The trials that beset you,
   the sorrows ye endure,
   are known to Christ your Saviour,
   whose perfect grace will cure.

6. O happy band of pilgrims,
   let fear not dim your eyes,
   remember, your afflictions
   shall lead to such a prize!

170 John Ernest Bode (1816-1874)

1. O Jesus, I have promised
   to serve thee to the end;
   be thou for ever near me,
   my Master and my friend:
   I shall not fear the battle
   if thou art by my side,
   nor wander from the pathway
   if thou wilt be my guide.

2. O let me feel thee near me;
   the world is ever near;
   I see the sights that dazzle,
   the tempting sounds I hear;
   my foes are ever near me,
   around me and within;
   but, Jesus, draw thou nearer,
   and shield my soul from sin.

3. O let me hear thee speaking
   in accents clear and still,
   above the storms of passion,
   the murmurs of self-will;
   O speak to reassure me,
   to hasten or control;
   O speak and make me listen,
   thou guardian of my soul.

4. O Jesus, thou hast promised,
   to all who follow thee,
   that where thou art in glory
   there shall thy servant be;
   and, Jesus, I have promised
   to serve thee to the end:
   O give me grace to follow,
   my Master and my friend.

5. O let me see thy foot-marks,
   and in them plant mine own;
   my hope to follow duly
   is in thy strength alone:
   O guide me, call me, draw me,
   uphold me to the end;
   and then in heav'n receive me,
   my Saviour and my friend.

171 Phillips Brooks (1835-1893) alt.

1. O little town of Bethlehem,
   how still we see thee lie!
   Above thy deep and dreamless sleep
   the silent stars go by.
   Yet in thy dark streets shineth
   the everlasting light;
   the hopes and fears of all the years
   are met in thee tonight.

2. O morning stars, together
   proclaim the holy birth,
   and praises sing to God the King,
   and peace to all the earth.
   For Christ is born of Mary;
   and, gathered all above,
   while mortals sleep, the angels keep
   their watch of wond'ring love;

3. How silently, how silently,
   the wondrous gift is giv'n!
   So God imparts to human hearts
   the blessings of his heav'n.
   No ear may hear his coming;
   but in this world of sin,
   where meek souls will receive him still,
   the dear Christ enters in.

4. O holy child of Bethlehem,
   descend to us, we pray;
   cast out our sin, and enter in,
   be born in us today.
   We hear the Christmas angels
   the great glad tidings tell:
   O come to us, abide with us,
   our Lord Emmanuel.

172 Stuart K. Hine (1899-1989)
© 1953 Stuart K. Hine/The Stuart Hine Trust/
Published by Kingsway Music (World, excl. N. &
S. America)

1. O Lord, my God!
   when I in awesome wonder
   consider all the works
   thy hand hath made;
   I see the stars,
   I hear the mighty thunder,
   thy pow'r throughout
   the universe displayed.

   Then sings my soul,
   my Saviour God, to thee,
   how great thou art! how great thou art!
   Then sings my soul,
   my Saviour God, to thee,
   how great thou art! how great thou art!

2. When through the woods
   and forest glades I wander
   and hear the birds sing
   sweetly in the trees;
   when I look down
   from lofty mountain grandeur,
   and hear the brook,
   and feel the gentle breeze.

3. And when I think that God,
   his Son not sparing,
   sent him to die,
   I scarce can take it in:
   that on the cross,
   my burden gladly bearing,
   he bled and died
   to take away my sin.

4. When Christ shall come
   with shout of acclamation
   and take me home,
   what joy shall fill my heart!
   Then shall I bow
   in humble adoration,
   and there proclaim,
   my God how great thou art!

173 George Matheson (1842-1906)

1. O Love that wilt not let me go,
   I rest my weary soul in thee;
   I give thee back the life I owe,
   that in thine ocean depths its flow
   may richer, fuller be.

2. O Light that follow'st all my way,
   I yield my flick'ring torch to thee;
   my heart restores its borrowed ray,
   that in thy sunshine's blaze its day
   may brighter, fairer be.

3. O Joy that seekest me through pain,
   I cannot close my heart to thee;
   I trace the rainbow through the rain,
   and feel the promise is not vain
   that morn shall tearless be.

4. O Cross that liftest up my head,
   I dare not ask to fly from thee:
   I lay in dust life's glory dead,
   and from the ground there blossoms red
   life that shall endless be.

174 George Bennard (1873-1958)
© The Rodeheaver Co./ Word Music
Administered by CopyCare

1. On a hill far away
   stood an old rugged cross,
   the emblem of suff'ring and shame;
   and I loved that old cross
   where the dearest and best
   for a world of lost sinners was slain.

Continued overleaf

So I'll cherish the old rugged cross,
till my trophies at last I lay down;
I will cling to the old rugged cross
and exchange it some day for a crown.

2. O that old rugged cross,
   so despised by the world,
   has a wondrous attraction for me:
   for the dear Lamb of God
   left his glory above
   to bear it to dark Calvary.

3. In the old rugged cross,
   stained with blood so divine,
   a wondrous beauty I see.
   For t'was on that old cross
   Jesus suffered and died
   to pardon and sanctify me.

4. To the old rugged cross
   I will ever be true,
   its shame and reproach gladly bear.
   Then he'll call me some day
   to my home far away;
   there his glory for ever I'll share.

175 Cecil Frances Alexander (1818-1895) alt.
© *This version 1996 Kevin Mayhew Ltd.*

1. Once in royal David's city
   stood a lowly cattle shed,
   where a mother laid her baby
   in a manger for his bed;
   Mary was that mother mild,
   Jesus Christ her little child.

2. He came down to earth from heaven,
   who is God and Lord of all,
   and his shelter was a stable,
   and his cradle was a stall;
   with the needy, poor and lowly,
   lived on earth our Saviour holy.

3. For he is our childhood's pattern,
   day by day like us he grew;
   he was little, weak and helpless,
   tears and smiles like us he knew;
   and he feeleth for our sadness,
   and he shareth in our gladness.

4. And our eyes at last shall see him
   through his own redeeming love,
   for that child so dear and gentle
   is our Lord in heav'n above;
   and he leads his children on
   to the place where he is gone.

176 William Bright (1824-1901)

1. Once, only once, and once for all,
   his precious life he gave;
   before the Cross our spirits fall,
   and own it strong to save.

2. 'One off'ring, single and complete,'
   with lips and heart we say;
   but what he never can repeat
   he shows forth day by day.

3. For, as the priest of Aaron's line
   within the holiest stood,
   and sprinkled all the mercy-shrine
   with sacrificial blood;

4. So he who once atonement wrought,
   our Priest of endless pow'r,
   presents himself for those he bought
   in that dark noontide hour.

5. And so we show thy death, O Lord,
   till thou again appear;
   and feel, when we approach thy board,
   we have an altar here.

6. All glory to the Father be,
   all glory to the Son,
   all glory, Holy Ghost, to thee,
   while endless ages run.

177 Traditional English carol, alt.

1. On Christmas night all Christians sing,
   to hear the news the angels bring,
   on Christmas night all Christians sing,
   to hear the news the angels bring.
   news of great joy, news of great mirth,
   news of our merciful King's birth.

2. Then why should we on earth be so sad,
   since our Redeemer made us glad,
   then why should we on earth be so sad,
   since our Redeemer made us glad,
   when from our sin he set us free,
   all for to gain our liberty?

3. When sin departs before his grace,
   then life and health come in its place,
   when sin departs before his grace,
   then life and health come in its place,
   angels and earth with joy may sing,
   all for to see the new-born King.

4. All out of darkness we have light,
   which made the angels sing this night:
   all out of darkness we have light,
   which made the angels sing this night:
   'Glory to God and peace to men,
   now and for evermore. Amen.'

178 Sydney Carter (b. 1915)
© 1971 Stainer & Bell Ltd.

1. One more step along the world I go,
   one more step along the world I go.
   From the old things to the new
   keep me travelling along with you.

   *And it's from the old
   I travel to the new,
   keep me travelling
   along with you.*

2. Round the corners of the world I turn,
   more and more about the world
      I learn.
   All the new things that I see
   you'll be looking at along with me.

3. As I travel through the bad and good,
   keep me travelling the way I should.
   Where I see no way to go,
   you'll be telling me the way, I know.

4. Give me courage when the world
      is rough,
   keep me loving though the world
      is tough.
   Leap and sing in all I do,
   keep me travelling along with you.

5. You are older than the world can be,
   you are younger than the life in me.
   Ever old and ever new,
   keep me travelling along with you.

179 18th century trans. Henry Williams Baker
(1821-1877) adapted by the editors of 'English Praise'
© Oxford University Press

1. On this day, the first of days,
   God the Father's name we praise,
   who, creation's Lord and spring,
   did the world from darkness bring.

2. On this day his only Son
   over death the triumph won;
   on this day the Spirit came
   with his gifts of living flame.

3. On this day his people raise
   one pure sacrifice of praise,
   and, with all the saints above,
   tell of Christ's redeeming love.

4. Praise, O God, to thee be giv'n,
   praise on earth and praise in heav'n,
   praise to thy eternal Son,
   who this day our vict'ry won.

180
Henry Williams Baker (1821-1877)
based on Psalms 148 and 150, alt.

1. O praise ye the Lord!
   praise him in the height;
   rejoice in his word, ye angels of light;
   ye heavens, adore him,
   by whom ye were made,
   and worship before him,
   in brightness arrayed.

2. O praise ye the Lord!
   praise him upon earth,
   in tuneful accord, all you of new birth;
   praise him who hath brought you
   his grace from above,
   praise him who hath taught you
   to sing of his love.

3. O praise ye the Lord!
   all things that give sound;
   each jubilant chord re-echo around;
   loud organs his glory
   forth tell in deep tone,
   and, sweet harp, the story
   of what he hath done.

4. O praise ye the Lord!
   thanksgiving and song
   to him be outpoured all ages along:
   for love in creation,
   for heaven restored,
   for grace of salvation,
   O praise ye the Lord!

181
Paul Gerhardt, trans. Robert Bridges

1. O sacred head sore wounded,
   defiled and put to scorn;
   O kingly head surrounded
   with mocking crown of thorn:
   what sorrow mars thy grandeur?
   Can death thy bloom de-flower?
   O countenance whose splendour
   the hosts of heav'n adore.

2. Thy beauty, long-desirèd,
   hath vanished from our sight;
   thy pow'r is all expirèd,
   and quenched the light of light.
   Ah me, for whom thou diest,
   hide not so far thy grace:
   show me, O love most highest,
   the brightness of thy face.

3. I pray thee, Jesus, own me,
   me, shepherd good, for thine;
   who to thy fold hast won me,
   and fed with truth divine.
   Me guilty, me refuse not,
   incline thy face to me,
   this comfort that I lose not,
   on earth to comfort thee.

4. In thy most bitter passion
   my heart to share doth cry,
   with thee for my salvation
   upon the cross to die.
   Ah, keep my heart thus movèd,
   to stand thy cross beneath,
   to mourn thee, well-belovèd,
   yet thank thee for thy death.

5. My days are few, O fail not,
   with thine immortal power,
   to hold me that I quail not
   in death's most fearful hour:
   that I may fight befriended,
   and see in my last strife
   to me thine arms extended
   upon the cross of life.

182
St Ambrose (c. 340-397) trans. John Ellerton (1826-1893) and Fenton John Anthony Hort (1828-1892)

1. O strength and stay upholding all
      creation,
   who ever dost thyself unmoved abide,
   yet day by day the light in due gradation
   from hour to hour through all its changes
      guide.

2. Grant to life's day a calm unclouded
     ending,
   an eve untouched by shadows of decay,
   the brightness of a holy death-bed
     blending
   with dawning glories of th'eternal day.

3. Hear us, O Father, gracious and
     forgiving,
   through Jesus Christ thy co-eternal Word,
   who with the Holy Ghost by all things
     living
   now and to endless ages art adored.

183 Charles Wesley (1707-1788) based on Leviticus 6:13

1. O thou who camest from above
   the fire celestial to impart,
   kindle a flame of sacred love
   on the mean altar of my heart.

2. There let it for thy glory burn
   with inextinguishable blaze,
   and trembling to its source return
   in humble prayer and fervent praise.

3. Jesus, confirm my heart's desire
   to work and speak and think for thee;
   still let me guard the holy fire
   and still stir up the gift in me.

4. Ready for all thy perfect will,
   my acts of faith and love repeat,
   till death thy endless mercies seal,
   and make the sacrifice complete.

184 Robert Grant (1779-1838), based on Psalm 104

1. O worship the King
   all glorious above;
   O gratefully sing
   his pow'r and his love:
   our shield and defender,
   the Ancient of Days,
   pavilioned in splendour,
   and girded with praise.

2. O tell of his might,
   O sing of his grace,
   whose robe is the light,
   whose canopy space;
   his chariots of wrath
   the deep thunder-clouds form,
   and dark in his path
   on the wings of the storm.

3. This earth, with its store
   of wonders untold,
   almighty, thy pow'r
   hath founded of old:
   hath stablished it fast
   by a changeless decree,
   and round it hath cast,
   like a mantle, the sea.

4. Thy bountiful care
   what tongue can recite?
   It breathes in the air,
   it shines in the light;
   it streams from the hills,
   it descends to the plain,
   and sweetly distils
   in the dew and the rain.

5. Frail children of dust,
   and feeble as frail,
   in thee do we trust,
   nor find thee to fail;
   thy mercies how tender,
   how firm to the end!
   Our maker, defender,
   redeemer, and friend.

6. O measureless might,
   ineffable love,
   while angels delight
   to hymn thee above,
   thy humbler creation,
   though feeble their lays,
   with true adoration
   shall sing to thy praise.

185 John Samuel Bewley Monsell (1811-1875)

1. O worship the Lord
   in the beauty of holiness;
   bow down before him,
   his glory proclaim;
   with gold of obedience
   and incense of lowliness,
   kneel and adore him:
   the Lord is his name.

2. Low at his feet lay
   thy burden of carefulness:
   high on his heart
   he will bear it for thee,
   comfort thy sorrows,
   and answer thy prayerfulness,
   guiding thy steps
   as may best for thee be.

3. Fear not to enter
   his courts in the slenderness
   of the poor wealth
   thou wouldst reckon as thine:
   truth in its beauty,
   and love in its tenderness,
   these are the off'rings
   to lay on his shrine.

4. These, though we bring them
   in trembling and fearfulness,
   he will accept
   for the name that is dear;
   mornings of joy give
   for evenings of tearfulness,
   trust for our trembling
   and hope for our fear.

186 Kevin Mayhew (b. 1942)
© 1976 Kevin Mayhew Ltd.

1. Peace, perfect peace
   is the gift of Christ our Lord.
   Peace, perfect peace,
   is the gift of Christ our Lord.
   Thus says the Lord,
   will the world know my friends.
   Peace, perfect peace,
   is the gift of Christ our Lord.

2. Love, perfect love . . .

3. Faith, perfect faith . . .

4. Hope, perfect hope . . .

5. Joy, perfect joy . . .

187 Unknown

1. Praise him, praise him,
   praise him in the morning,
   praise him in the noontime.
   Praise him, praise him,
   praise him when the sun goes down.

2. Love him, love him, . . .

3. Trust him, trust him, . . .

4. Serve him, serve him, . . .

5. Jesus, Jesus, . . .

188 Henry Francis Lyte (1793-1847), based on Psalm 103

1. Praise, my soul, the King of heaven!
   To his feet thy tribute bring;
   ransomed, healed, restored, forgiven,
   who like me his praise should sing?
   Praise him! Praise him!
   Praise him! Praise him!
   Praise the everlasting King!

2. Praise him for his grace and favour
   to our fathers in distress;
   praise him still the same as ever,
   slow to chide and swift to bless.
   Praise him! Praise him!
   Praise him! Praise him!
   Glorious in his faithfulness!

3. Father-like, he tends and spares us;
   well our feeble frame he knows;
   in his hands he gently bears us,
   rescues us from all our foes.
   Praise him! Praise him!
   Praise him! Praise him!
   Widely as his mercy flows!

4. Angels, help us to adore him;
   ye behold him face to face;
   sun and moon, bow down before him,
   dwellers all in time and space.
   Praise him! Praise him!
   Praise him! Praise him!
   Praise with us the God of grace!

189 vs 1 and 2 from 'Foundling Hospital Collection' (1796)
vs 3 Edward Osler (1798-1863)

1. Praise the Lord, ye heav'ns, adore him!
   Praise him, angels, in the height;
   sun and moon, rejoice before him,
   praise him, all ye stars and light.
   Praise the Lord, for he hath spoken;
   worlds his mighty voice obeyed:
   laws, which never shall be broken,
   for their guidance he hath made.

2. Praise the Lord, for he is glorious:
   never shall his promise fail.
   God hath made his saints victorious;
   sin and death shall not prevail.
   Praise the God of our salvation,
   hosts on high, his pow'r proclaim;
   heav'n and earth and all creation,
   laud and magnify his name!

3. Worship, honour, glory, blessing,
   Lord, we offer to thy name;
   young and old, thy praise expressing,
   join their Saviour to proclaim.
   As the saints in heav'n adore thee,
   we would bow before thy throne;
   as thine angels serve before thee,
   so on earth thy will be done.

190 John Henry Newman (1801-1890)

1. Praise to the Holiest in the height,
   and in the depth be praise;
   in all his words most wonderful,
   most sure in all his ways.

2. O loving wisdom of our God!
   when all was sin and shame,
   a second Adam to the fight,
   and to the rescue came.

3. O wisest love! that flesh and blood,
   which did in Adam fail,
   should strive afresh against the foe,
   should strive and should prevail.

4. And that a higher gift than grace
   should flesh and blood refine,
   God's presence and his very self,
   and essence all-divine.

5. And in the garden secretly,
   and on the cross on high,
   should teach his brethren, and inspire
   to suffer and to die.

6. Praise to the Holiest in the height,
   and in the depth be praise;
   in all his words most wonderful,
   most sure in all his ways.

191 Joachim Neander (1650-1680)
trans. Catherine Winkworth (1827-1878)

1. Praise to the Lord,
   the Almighty, the King of creation!
   O my soul, praise him,
   for he is thy health and salvation.
   All ye who hear,
   now to his temple draw near;
   joining in glad adoration.

Continued overleaf

2. Praise to the Lord,
   who o'er all things so wondrously reigneth,
   shieldeth thee gently from harm,
   or when fainting sustaineth:
   hast thou not seen
   how thy heart's wishes have been
   granted in what he ordaineth?

3. Praise to the Lord,
   who doth prosper thy work and defend thee,
   surely his goodness and mercy
   shall daily attend thee:
   ponder anew
   what the Almighty can do,
   if to the end he befriend thee.

4. Praise to the Lord,
   O let all that is in us adore him!
   All that hath life and breath,
   come now with praises before him.
   Let the 'Amen'
   sound from his people again,
   gladly for ay we adore him.

192 Paul Gerhardt (1607-1676)
trans. John Wesley (1703-1791) and others

1. Put thou thy trust in God,
   in duty's path go on;
   walk in his strength with faith and hope,
   so shall thy work be done.

2. Commit thy ways to him,
   thy works into his hands,
   and rest on his unchanging word,
   who heav'n and earth commands.

3. Though years on years roll on,
   his cov'nant shall endure;
   though clouds and darkness hide his path,
   the promised grace is sure.

4. Give to the winds thy fears;
   hope, and be undismayed:
   God hears thy sighs and counts thy tears;
   God shall lift up thy head.

5. Through waves and clouds and storms
   his pow'r will clear thy way:
   wait thou his time; the darkest night
   shall end in brightest day.

6. Leave to his sov'reign sway
   to choose and to command;
   so shalt thou, wond'ring, own his way,
   how wise, how strong his hand.

193 Robert Bridges (1844-1930)

1. Rejoice, O land, in God thy might;
   his will obey, him serve aright;
   for thee the saints uplift their voice:
   fear not, O land, in God rejoice.

2. Glad shalt thou be, with blessing
      crowned,
   with joy and peace thou shalt abound;
   yea, love with thee shall make his home
   until thou see God's kingdom come.

3. He shall forgive thy sins untold:
   remember thou his love of old;
   walk in his way, his word adore,
   and keep his truth for evermore.

194 Charles Wesley (1707-1788)

1. Rejoice the Lord is King!
   Your Lord and King adore;
   mortals, give thanks and sing,
   and triumph evermore.

   Lift up your heart, lift up your voice;
   rejoice, again I say, rejoice.

2. Jesus the Saviour reigns,
   the God of truth and love;
   when he had purged our stains,
   he took his seat above.

3. His kingdom cannot fail;
   he rules o'er earth and heav'n;
   the keys of death and hell
   are to our Jesus giv'n.

4. He sits at God's right hand
   till all his foes submit,
   and bow to his command,
   and fall beneath his feet.

195 Henry Hart Milman (1791-1868), alt.

1. Ride on, ride on in majesty!
   Hark all the tribes hosanna cry;
   thy humble beast pursues his road
   with palms and scattered garments
      strowed.

2. Ride on, ride on in majesty!
   In lowly pomp ride on to die;
   O Christ, thy triumphs now begin
   o'er captive death and conquered sin.

3. Ride on, ride on in majesty!
   The wingèd squadrons of the sky
   look down with sad and wond'ring eyes
   to see th'approaching sacrifice.

4. Ride on, ride on in majesty!
   Thy last and fiercest strife is nigh;
   the Father, on his sapphire throne,
   awaits his own appointed Son.

5. Ride on, ride on in majesty!
   In lowly pomp ride on to die;
   bow thy meek head to mortal pain,
   then take, O God, thy pow'r, and reign.

196 Augustus Montague Toplady (1740-1778) alt.

1. Rock of ages, cleft for me,
   let me hide myself in thee;
   let the water and the blood,
   from thy riven side which flowed,
   be of sin the double cure:
   cleanse me from its guilt and pow'r.

2. Not the labours of my hands
   can fulfil thy law's demands;
   could my zeal no respite know,
   could my tears for ever flow,
   all for sin could not atone:
   thou must save, and thou alone.

3. Nothing in my hands I bring,
   simply to thy cross I cling;
   naked, come to thee for dress;
   helpless, look to thee for grace;
   tainted, to the fountain fly;
   wash me, Saviour, or I die.

4. While I draw this fleeting breath,
   when mine eyelids close in death,
   when I soar through tracts unknown,
   see thee on thy judgement throne;
   Rock of ages, cleft for me,
   let me hide myself in thee.

197 John Ellerton (1826-1893)

1. Saviour, again
   to thy dear name we raise
   with one accord
   our parting hymn of praise;
   we stand to bless thee
   ere our worship cease;
   then, lowly kneeling,
   wait thy word of peace.

2. Grant us thy peace
   upon our homeward way;
   with thee began,
   with thee shall end, the day:
   guard thou the lips from sin,
   the hearts from shame,
   that in this house
   have called upon thy name.

Continued overleaf

3. Grant us thy peace,
Lord, through the coming night;
turn thou for us
its darkness into light;
from harm and danger
keep thy children free,
for dark and light
are both alike to thee.

4. Grant us thy peace
throughout our earthly life,
our balm in sorrow,
and our stay in strife;
then, when thy voice
shall bid our conflict cease,
call us, O Lord,
to thine eternal peace.

198 Edward Caswall (1814-1878)

1. See, amid the winter's snow,
born for us on earth below,
see, the tender Lamb appears,
promised from eternal years.

Hail, thou ever-blessèd morn,
hail, redemption's happy dawn!
Sing through all Jerusalem,
Christ is born in Bethlehem.

2. Lo, within a manger lies
he who built the starry skies;
he, who, throned in heights sublime,
sits amid the cherubim.

3. Say, you holy shepherds, say,
what your joyful news today?
Wherefore have you left your sheep
on the lonely mountain steep?

4. 'As we watched at dead of night,
there appeared a wondrous light;
angels, singing peace on earth,
told us of the Saviour's birth.'

5. Sacred infant, all divine,
what a tender love was thine,
thus to come from highest bliss,
down to such a world as this!

6. Virgin mother, Mary, blest,
by the joys that fill thy breast,
pray for us, that we may prove
worthy of the Saviour's love.

199 Michael Perry (1942-1996)
© 1965 Mrs B. Perry/Jubilate Hymns

1. See him lying on a bed of straw:
a draughty stable with an open door.
Mary cradling the babe she bore:
the Prince of Glory is his name.

O now carry me to Bethlehem
to see the Lord of Love again:
just as poor as was the stable then,
the Prince of Glory when he came!

2. Star of silver, sweep across the skies,
show where Jesus in the manger lies;
shepherds, swiftly from your stupor rise
to see the Saviour of the world!

3. Angels, sing again the song you sang,
sing the glory of God's gracious plan;
sing that Bethlehem's little baby can
be the Saviour of us all.

4. Mine are riches, from your poverty;
from your innocence, eternity;
mine, forgiveness by your death for me,
child of sorrow for my joy.

200 Joseph Mohr, (1792-1848)
trans. John Freeman Young (1820-1885)

1. Silent night, holy night.
All is calm, all is bright,
round yon virgin mother and child;
holy infant, so tender and mild,
sleep in heavenly peace,
sleep in heavenly peace.

2. Silent night, holy night.
   Shepherds quake at the sight,
   glories stream from heaven afar,
   heav'nly hosts sing alleluia:
   Christ, the Saviour is born,
   Christ, the Saviour is born.

3. Silent night, holy night.
   Son of God, love's pure light,
   radiant beams from thy holy face,
   with the dawn of redeeming grace:
   Jesus, Lord, at thy birth,
   Jesus, Lord, at thy birth.

201 Charles Wesley (1707-1788)
based on Ephesians 6:10-18

1. Soldiers of Christ, arise,
   and put your armour on,
   strong in the strength which God supplies
   through his eternal Son.

2. Strong in the Lord of hosts,
   and in his mighty pow'r;
   who in the strength of Jesus trusts
   is more than conqueror.

3. Stand then in his great might,
   with all his strength endued;
   and take, to arm you for the fight,
   the panoply of God.

4. To keep your armour bright,
   attend with constant care,
   still walking in your Captain's sight
   and watching unto prayer.

5. From strength to strength go on,
   wrestle and fight and pray;
   tread all the pow'rs of darkness down,
   and win the well-fought day.

6. That, having all things done,
   and all your conflicts past,
   ye may o'ercome, through Christ alone,
   and stand entire at last.

202 Christopher Wordsworth (1807-1885)

1. Songs of thankfulness and praise,
   Jesus, Lord to thee we raise,
   manifested by the star
   to the sages from afar;
   branch of royal David's stem,
   in thy birth at Bethlehem;
   anthems be to thee addressed:
   God in man made manifest.

2. Manifest at Jordan's stream,
   prophet, priest and King supreme,
   and at Cana wedding-guest,
   in thy Godhead manifest,
   manifest in pow'r divine,
   changing water into wine;
   anthems be to thee addressed:
   God in man made manifest.

3. Manifest in making whole,
   palsied limbs and fainting soul,
   manifest in valiant fight,
   quelling all the devil's might,
   manifest in gracious will,
   ever bringing good from ill;
   anthems be to thee addressed:
   God in man made manifest.

4. Sun and moon shall darkened be,
   stars shall fall, the heav'ns shall flee;
   Christ will then like lightning shine,
   all will see his glorious sign.
   All will then the trumpet hear,
   all will see the judge appear;
   thou by all wilt be confessed:
   God in man made manifest.

5. Grant us grace to see thee, Lord,
   mirrored in thy holy word;
   may we imitate thee now,
   and be pure, as pure art thou;
   that we like to thee may be
   at thy great Epiphany,
   and may praise thee, ever blest,
   God in man made manifest.

203

Daniel Iverson (1890-1972)
© 1963 Birdwing Music/EMI Christian Music
Publishing. Administered by CopyCare

1. Spirit of the living God, fall afresh on me.
   Spirit of the living God, fall afresh on me.
   Melt me, mould me, fill me, use me.
   Spirit of the living God, fall afresh on me.

2. Spirit of the living God, fall afresh on us.
   Spirit of the living God, fall afresh on us.
   Melt us, mould us, fill us, use us.
   Spirit of the living God, fall afresh on us.

   When appropriate a third verse may be
   added, singing 'on them', for example,
   before Confirmation, or at a service for the
   sick.

204

James Montgomery (1771-1854)

1. Stand up and bless the Lord,
   ye people of his choice;
   stand up and bless the Lord your God
   with heart and soul and voice.

2. Though high above all praise,
   above all blessing high,
   who would not fear his holy name,
   and laud and magnify?

3. O for the living flame
   from his own altar brought,
   to touch our lips, our mind inspire,
   and wing to heav'n our thought.

4. God is our strength and song,
   and his salvation ours;
   then be his love in Christ proclaimed
   with all our ransomed pow'rs.

5. Stand up and bless the Lord,
   the Lord your God adore;
   stand up and bless his glorious name
   henceforth for evermore.

205

Jean Holloway (b. 1939)
© 1996 Kevin Mayhew Ltd.

1. Stand up, stand up for Jesus,
   stand up before his cross,
   an instrument of torture
   inflicting pain and loss;
   transformed by his obedience
   to God's redeeming plan,
   the cross was overpowered
   by Christ, both God and man.

2. Stand up, stand up for Jesus,
   be counted as his own;
   his gospel of forgiveness
   he cannot spread alone.
   The love which draws us to him,
   he calls us out to share;
   he calls us to the margins
   to be his presence there.

3. Stand up, stand up for Jesus,
   in faith and hope be strong,
   stand firm for right and justice,
   opposed to sin and wrong.
   Give comfort to the wounded,
   and care for those in pain,
   for Christ, in those who suffer,
   is crucified again.

4. Stand up, stand up for Jesus,
   who reigns as King of kings,
   be ready for the challenge
   of faith his kingship brings.
   He will not force obedience,
   he gives to each the choice
   to turn from all that's holy,
   or in his love rejoice.

5. Stand up, stand up for Jesus,
   give courage to the weak,
   be unashamed to praise him,
   be bold his name to speak.
   Confront the cross unflinching,
   Christ's love has set us free;
   he conquered death for ever
   and lives eternally.

206

Graham Kendrick (b. 1950)
© 1988 Make Way Music

1. Such love, pure as the whitest snow;
   such love weeps for the shame I know;
   such love, paying the debt I owe;
   O Jesus, such love.

2. Such love, stilling my restlessness;
   such love, filling my emptiness;
   such love, showing me holiness;
   O Jesus, such love.

3. Such love springs from eternity;
   such love, streaming through history;
   such love, fountain of life to me;
   O Jesus, such love.

207

John Keble (1792-1866)

1. Sun of my soul, thou Saviour dear,
   it is not night if thou be near:
   O may no earth-born cloud arise
   to hide thee from thy servant's eyes.

2. When the soft dews of kindly sleep
   my wearied eyelids gently steep,
   be my last thought, how sweet to rest
   for ever on my Saviour's breast.

3. Abide with me from morn till eve,
   for without thee I cannot live;
   abide with me when night is nigh,
   for without thee I dare not die.

4. Watch by the sick; enrich the poor
   with blessings from thy boundless store;
   be ev'ry mourner's sleep tonight
   like infant's slumbers, pure and light.

208

Charles William Everest (1814-1877)
based on Mark 8, alt.

1. Take up thy cross, the Saviour said,
   if thou wouldst my disciple be;
   deny thyself, the world forsake,
   and humbly follow after me.

2. Take up thy cross – let not its weight
   fill thy weak spirit with alarm:
   his strength shall bear thy spirit up,
   and brace thy heart, and nerve thine arm.

3. Take up thy cross, nor heed the shame,
   nor let thy foolish pride rebel:
   thy Lord for thee the Cross endured,
   to save thy soul from death and hell.

4. Take up thy cross then in his strength,
   and calmly ev'ry danger brave;
   'twill guide thee to a better home,
   and lead to vict'ry o'er the grave.

5. Take up thy cross, and follow Christ,
   nor think till death to lay it down;
   for only those who bear the cross
   may hope to wear the glorious crown.

6. To thee, great Lord, the One in Three,
   all praise for evermore ascend:
   O grant us in our home to see
   the heav'nly life that knows no end.

209

George Herbert (1593-1633)

1. Teach me, my God and King,
   in all things thee to see;
   and what I do in anything
   to do it as for thee.

2. A man that looks on glass,
   on it may stay his eye;
   or, if he pleaseth, through it pass,
   and then the heav'n espy.

3. All may of thee partake;
   nothing can be so mean
   which, with this tincture, 'For thy sake',
   will not grow bright and clean.

4. A servant with this clause
   makes drudgery divine;
   who sweeps a room, as for thy laws,
   makes that and the action fine.

Continued overleaf

5. This is the famous stone
   that turneth all to gold;
   for that which God doth touch and own
   cannot for less be told.

Timothy Dudley-Smith (b. 1926)
based on Luke 1:46-55
© 1961 Timothy Dudley-Smith

210

1. Tell out, my soul, the greatness of the Lord:
   unnumbered blessings, give my
      spirit voice;
   tender to me the promise of his word;
   in God my Saviour shall my heart rejoice.

2. Tell out, my soul, the greatness of
      his name:
   make known his might, the deeds his
      arm has done;
   his mercy sure, from age to age the same;
   his holy name, the Lord, the mighty one.

3. Tell out, my soul, the greatness of
      his might:
   pow'rs and dominions lay their glory by;
   proud hearts and stubborn wills are put
      to flight,
   the hungry fed, the humble lifted high.

4. Tell out, my soul, the glories of his word:
   firm is his promise, and his mercy sure.
   Tell out, my soul, the greatness of
      the Lord
   to children's children and for evermore.

211
Sabine Baring-Gould (1834-1924),
based on 'Birjina gaztettobat zegoen'

1. The angel Gabriel from heaven came,
   his wings as drifted snow, his eyes
      as flame.
   'All hail,' said he,
   'thou lowly maiden, Mary,
   most highly favoured lady.' Gloria!

2. 'For known a blessèd Mother thou
      shalt be.
   All generations laud and honour thee.
   Thy Son shall be Emmanuel,
   by seers foretold,
   most highly favoured lady.' Gloria!

3. Then gentle Mary meekly bowed
      her head.
   'To me be as it pleaseth God,' she said.
   'My soul shall laud and magnify
   his holy name.'
   Most highly favoured lady! Gloria!

4. Of her, Emmanuel, the Christ, was born
   in Bethlehem, all on a Christmas morn;
   and Christian folk throughout
   the world will ever say:
   'Most highly favoured lady.' Gloria!

212
Samuel John Stone (1839-1900)

1. The Church's one foundation
   is Jesus Christ, her Lord;
   she is his new creation,
   by water and the word;
   from heav'n he came and sought her
   to be his holy bride,
   with his own blood he bought her,
   and for her life he died.

2. Elect from ev'ry nation,
   yet one o'er all the earth,
   her charter of salvation,
   one Lord, one faith, one birth;
   one holy name she blesses,
   partakes one holy food,
   and to one hope she presses,
   with ev'ry grace endued.

3. 'Mid toil and tribulation,
   and tumult of her war,
   she waits the consummation
   of peace for evermore;
   till with the vision glorious
   her longing eyes are blest,
   and the great Church victorious
   shall be the Church at rest.

4. Yet she on earth hath union
   with God the Three in One,
   and mystic sweet communion
   with those whose rest is won:
   O happy ones and holy! Lord,
   give us grace that we
   like them, the meek and lowly,
   on high may dwell with thee.

213 St John of Damascus (c. 750)
trans. John Mason Neale (1818-1866)

1. The day of resurrection!
   Earth, tell it out abroad;
   the passover of gladness,
   the passover of God!
   From death to life eternal,
   from earth unto the sky,
   our Christ hath brought us over
   with hymns of victory.

2. Our hearts be pure from evil,
   that we may see aright
   the Lord in rays eternal
   of resurrection-light;
   and list'ning to his accents,
   may hear so calm and plain
   his own 'All hail' and, hearing,
   may raise the victor strain.

3. Now let the heav'ns be joyful,
   and earth her song begin,
   the round world keep high triumph,
   and all that is therein;
   let all things, seen and unseen,
   their notes of gladness blend,
   for Christ the Lord hath risen,
   our joy that hath no end.

214 John Ellerton (1826-1893)

1. The day thou gavest, Lord, is ended:
   the darkness falls at thy behest;
   to thee our morning hymns ascended;
   thy praise shall sanctify our rest.

2. We thank thee that thy Church unsleeping,
   while earth rolls onward into light,
   through all the world her watch
       is keeping,
   and rests not now by day or night.

3. As o'er each continent and island
   the dawn leads on another day,
   the voice of prayer is never silent,
   nor dies the strain of praise away.

4. The sun that bids us rest is waking
   our brethren 'neath the western sky,
   and hour by hour fresh lips are making
   thy wondrous doings heard on high.

5. So be it, Lord; thy throne shall never,
   like earth's proud empires, pass away;
   thy kingdom stands, and grows for ever,
   till all thy creatures own thy sway.

215 From William Sandys' 'Christmas Carols,
Ancient and Modern', alt.

1. The first Nowell the angel did say
   was to certain poor shepherds in fields as
       they lay:
   in fields where they lay keeping their sheep,
   on a cold winter's night that was so deep.

   *Nowell, Nowell, Nowell, Nowell,
   born is the King of Israel!*

2. They lookèd up and saw a star,
   shining in the east, beyond them far,
   and to the earth it gave great light,
   and so it continued both day and night.

Continued overleaf

3. And by the light of that same star,
   three wise men came from country far;
   to seek for a king was their intent,
   and to follow the star wherever it went.

   Nowell, Nowell, Nowell, Nowell,
   born is the King of Israel!

4. This star drew nigh to the north-west,
   o'er Bethlehem it took its rest,
   and there it did both stop and stay
   right over the place where Jesus lay.

5. Then entered in those wise men three,
   full rev'rently upon their knee,
   and offered there in his presence,
   their gold and myrrh and frankincense.

6. Then let us all with one accord
   sing praises to our heav'nly Lord,
   who with the Father we adore
   and Spirit blest for evermore.

216 Thomas Kelly (1769-1855)

1. The head that once was crowned
       with thorns
   is crowned with glory now:
   a royal diadem adorns
   the mighty victor's brow.

2. The highest place that heav'n affords
   is his, is his by right.
   The King of kings and Lord of lords,
   and heav'ns eternal light.

3. The joy of all who dwell above,
   the joy of all below,
   to whom he manifests his love,
   and grants his name to know.

4. To them the cross, with all its shame,
   with all its grace is giv'n;
   their name an everlasting name,
   their joy the joy of heav'n.

5. They suffer with their Lord below,
   they reign with him above,
   their profit and their joy to know
   the myst'ry of his love.

6. The cross he bore is life and health,
   though shame and death to him;
   his people's hope, his people's wealth,
   their everlasting theme.

217 Henry Williams Baker (1821-1877), based on Psalm 23

1. The King of love my shepherd is,
   whose goodness faileth never;
   I nothing lack if I am his
   and he is mine for ever.

2. Where streams of living water flow
   my ransomed soul he leadeth,
   and where the verdant pastures grow
   with food celestial feedeth.

3. Perverse and foolish oft I strayed,
   but yet in love he sought me,
   and on his shoulder gently laid,
   and home, rejoicing, brought me.

4. In death's dark vale I fear no ill
   with thee, dear Lord, beside me;
   thy rod and staff my comfort still,
   thy cross before to guide me.

5. Thou spread'st a table in my sight,
   thy unction grace bestoweth:
   and O what transport of delight
   from thy pure chalice floweth!

6. And so through all the length of days
   thy goodness faileth never;
   good Shepherd, may I sing thy praise
   within thy house for ever.

218 Psalm 23 from 'The Scottish Psalter' (1650)

1. The Lord's my shepherd, I'll not want.
   He makes me down to lie
   in pastures green.
   He leadeth me the quiet waters by.

2. My soul he doth restore again,
   and me to walk doth make
   within the paths of righteousness,
   e'en for his own name's sake.

3. Yea, though I walk in death's dark vale,
   yet will I fear no ill.
   For thou art with me, and thy rod
   and staff me comfort still.

4. My table thou hast furnishèd
   in presence of my foes,
   my head thou dost with oil anoint,
   and my cup overflows.

5. Goodness and mercy all my life
   shall surely follow me.
   And in God's house for evermore
   my dwelling-place shall be.

219 Cecil Frances Alexander (1818-1895), alt.

1. There is a green hill far away,
   outside a city wall,
   where the dear Lord was crucified
   who died to save us all.

2. We may not know, we cannot tell
   what pains he had to bear,
   but we believe it was for us
   he hung and suffered there.

3. He died that we might be forgiv'n,
   he died to make us good;
   that we might go at last to heav'n,
   saved by his precious blood.

4. There was no other good enough
   to pay the price of sin;
   he only could unlock the gate
   of heav'n, and let us in.

5. O, dearly, dearly has he loved,
   and we must love him too,
   and trust in his redeeming blood,
   and try his works to do.

220

Melody Green, based on Scripture
© 1982 Birdwing/Music/BMG Songs Inc/
Ears to hear music/EMI Christian Music
Publishing/CopyCare Ltd

1. There is a Redeemer,
   Jesus, God's own Son,
   precious Lamb of God, Messiah,
   Holy One.

   Thank you, O my Father,
   for giving us your Son,
   and leaving your Spirit
   till the work on earth is done.

2. Jesus, my Redeemer,
   name above all names,
   precious Lamb of God, Messiah,
   O for sinners slain.

3. When I stand in glory,
   I will see his face,
   and there I'll serve my King for ever,
   in that holy place.

221 Damian Lundy (1944-1997)
© 1978, 1993 Kevin Mayhew Ltd.

1. The Spirit lives to set us free,
   walk, walk in the light.
   He binds us all in unity,
   walk, walk in the light.

   Walk in the light (x3)
   walk in the light of the Lord.

2. Jesus promised life to all,
   walk, walk in the light.
   The dead were wakened by his call,
   walk, walk in the light.

3. He died in pain on Calvary,
   walk, walk in the light,
   to save the lost like you and me,
   walk, walk in the light.

4. We know his death was not the end,
   walk, walk in the light.
   He gave his Spirit to be our friend,
   walk, walk in the light.

Continued overleaf

5. By Jesus' love our wounds are healed,
   walk, walk in the light.
   The Father's kindness is revealed,
   walk, walk in the light.

   Walk in the light (x3)
   walk in the light of the Lord.

6. The Spirit lives in you and me,
   walk, walk in the light.
   His light will shine for all to see,
   walk, walk in the light.

222 Latin hymn (17th century)
trans. Francis Pott (1832-1909)

1. The strife is o'er, the battle done;
   now is the Victor's triumph won;
   O let the song of praise be sung:
   Alleluia, alleluia, alleluia.

2. Death's mightiest pow'rs have done
      their worst,
   and Jesus hath his foes dispersed;
   let shouts of praise and joy outburst:
   Alleluia, alleluia, alleluia.

3. On the third morn he rose again
   glorious in majesty to reign;
   O let us swell the joyful strain:
   Alleluia, alleluia, alleluia.

4. Lord, by the stripes which wounded thee
   from death's dread sting thy servants free,
   that we may live, and sing to thee:
   Alleluia, alleluia, alleluia.

223 'A toi la gloire' Edmond Louis Budry (1854-1932)
trans. Richard Birch Hoyle
© Copyright Control

1. Thine be the glory,
   risen, conqu'ring Son,
   endless is the vict'ry
   thou o'er death hast won;
   angels in bright raiment
   rolled the stone away,
   kept the folded grave-clothes
   where thy body lay.

Thine be the glory,
   risen, conqu'ring Son,
endless is the vict'ry
   thou o'er death has won.

2. Lo! Jesus meets us,
   risen from the tomb;
   lovingly he greets us,
   scatters fear and gloom.
   Let the Church with gladness
   hymns of triumph sing,
   for her Lord now liveth;
   death hath lost its sting.

3. No more we doubt thee,
   glorious Prince of Life!
   Life is naught without thee:
   aid us in our strife.
   Make us more than conqu'rors
   through thy deathless love.
   Bring us safe through Jordan
   to thy home above.

224 Mary Fawler Maude (1819-1913) alt.

1. Thine for ever! God of love,
   hear us from thy throne above;
   thine for ever may we be
   here and in eternity.

2. Thine for ever! Lord of life,
   shield us through our earthly strife;
   thou the life, the truth, the way,
   guide us to the realms of day.

3. Thine for ever! O how blest
   they who find in thee their rest!
   Saviour, guardian, heav'nly friend,
   O defend us to the end.

4. Thine for ever! Shepherd, keep
   us thy frail and trembling sheep;
   safe within thy tender care,
   let us all thy goodness share.

5. Thine for ever! thou our guide,
   all our wants by thee supplied,
   all our sins by thee forgiv'n,
   lead us, Lord, from earth to heav'n.

225 Les Garrett (b. 1944)
© 1967 Scripture in Song/Integrity Music/
Sovereign Music UK

1. This is the day, this is the day
   that the Lord has made,
   that the Lord has made;
   we will rejoice, we will rejoice
   and be glad in it, and be glad in it.
   This is the day that the Lord has made;
   we will rejoice and be glad in it.
   This is the day, this is the day
   that the Lord has made.

2. This is the day, this is the day
   when he rose again,
   when he rose again;
   we will rejoice, we will rejoice
   and be glad in it, and be glad in it.
   This is the day when he rose again;
   we will rejoice and be glad in it.
   This is the day, this is the day
   when he rose again.

3. This is the day, this is the day
   when the Spirit came,
   when the Spirit came;
   we will rejoice, we will rejoice
   and be glad in it, and be glad in it.
   This is the day when the Spirit came;
   we will rejoice and be glad in it.
   This is the day, this is the day
   when the Spirit came.

226 George Ratcliffe Woodward (1848-1934)
© Copyright control

1. This joyful Eastertide,
   away with sin and sorrow.
   My love, the Crucified,
   hath sprung to life this morrow.

Had Christ, that once was slain,
ne'er burst his three-day prison,
our faith had been in vain:
but now hath Christ arisen,
arisen, arisen, arisen.

2. My flesh in hope shall rest,
   and for a season slumber;
   till trump from east to west
   shall wake the dead in number.

3. Death's flood hath lost its chill,
   since Jesus crossed the river:
   lover of souls, from ill
   my passing soul deliver.

227 Emily Elizabeth Steele Elliott (1836-1897)
based on Luke 2:7
adapted by Michael Forster (b. 1946)
© This version copyright 1996 Kevin Mayhew Ltd.

1. Thou didst leave thy throne
   and thy kingly crown
   when thou camest to earth for me,
   but in Bethlehem's home
   was there found no room
   for thy holy nativity.

   O come to my heart, Lord Jesus,
   there is room in my heart for thee.

2. Heaven's arches rang
   when the angels sang
   and proclaimed thee of royal degree,
   but in lowliest birth
   didst thou come to earth
   and in deepest humility.

3. Though the fox found rest,
   and the bird its nest
   in the shade of the cedar tree,
   yet the world found no bed
   for the Saviour's head
   in the desert of Galilee.

Continued overleaf

4. Though thou cam'st, Lord,
   with the living word
   that should set all thy people free,
   yet with treachery,
   scorn and a crown of thorn
   did they bear thee to Calvary.

   O come to my heart, Lord Jesus,
   there is room in my heart for thee.

5. When the heav'ns shall ring
   and the angels sing
   at thy coming to victory,
   let thy voice call me home,
   saying 'Heav'n has room,
   there is room at my side for thee.'

228 John Marriott (1780-1825) alt.

1. Thou, whose almighty word
   chaos and darkness heard,
   and took their flight;
   hear us, we humbly pray,
   and where the gospel day
   sheds not its glorious ray,
   let there be light.

2. Thou, who didst come to bring
   on thy redeeming wing,
   healing and sight,
   health to the sick in mind,
   sight to the inly blind,
   O now to humankind
   let there be light.

3. Spirit of truth and love,
   life-giving, holy Dove,
   speed forth thy flight;
   move on the water's face,
   bearing the lamp of grace,
   and in earth's darkest place
   let there be light.

4. Holy and blessèd Three,
   glorious Trinity,
   Wisdom, Love, Might;
   boundless as ocean's tide
   rolling in fullest pride,
   through the earth far and wide
   let there be light.

229 Psalm 34 in 'New Version' (Tate and Brady, 1696)

1. Through all the changing scenes of life,
   in trouble and in joy,
   the praises of my God shall still
   my heart and tongue employ.

2. O magnify the Lord with me,
   with me exalt his name;
   when in distress to him I called,
   he to my rescue came.

3. The hosts of God encamp around
   the dwellings of the just;
   deliv'rance he affords to all
   who on his succour trust.

4. O make but trial of his love:
   experience will decide
   how blest are they, and only they,
   who in his truth confide.

5. Fear him, ye saints, and you will then
   have nothing else to fear;
   make you his service your delight,
   your wants shall be his care.

6. To Father, Son and Holy Ghost,
   the God whom we adore,
   be glory as it was, is now,
   and shall be evermore.

230 Bernhardt Severin Ingemann (1789-1862) trans. Sabine Baring-Gould (1834-1924) alt.

1. Through the night of doubt and sorrow
   onward goes the pilgrim band,
   singing songs of expectation,
   marching to the promised land.

2. Clear before us, through the darkness,
  gleams and burns the guiding light;
  so we march in hope united,
  stepping fearless through the night.

3. One the light of God's own presence
  o'er his ransomed people shed,
  chasing far the gloom and terror,
  bright'ning all the path we tread.

4. One the object of our journey,
  one the faith which never tires,
  one the earnest looking forward,
  one the hope our God inspires.

5. One the strain that lips of thousands
  lift as from the heart of one:
  one the conflict, one the peril,
  one the march in God begun.

6. One the gladness of rejoicing
  on the far eternal shore,
  where the one almighty Father
  reigns in love for evermore.

7. Onward, therefore, fellow pilgrims,
  onward with the Cross our aid;
  bear its shame and fight its battle,
  till we rest beneath its shade.

8. Soon shall come the great awaking,
  soon the rending of the tomb;
  then the scatt'ring of all shadows,
  and the end of toil and gloom.

231 Edward Hayes Plumptre (1821-1891), alt.

1. Thy hand, O God, has guided
  thy flock, from age to age;
  the wondrous tale is written,
  full clear, on ev'ry page;
  our forebears owned thy goodness,
  and we their deeds record;
  and both of this bear witness:
  one Church, one Faith, one Lord.

2. Thy heralds brought glad tidings
  to greatest, as to least;
  they bade them rise, and hasten
  to share the great King's feast;
  and this was all their teaching,
  in ev'ry deed and word,
  to all alike proclaiming:
  one Church, one Faith, one Lord.

3. Through many a day of darkness,
  through many a scene of strife,
  the faithful few fought bravely
  to guard the nation's life.
  Their gospel of redemption,
  sin pardoned, hope restored,
  was all in this enfolded:
  one Church, one Faith, one Lord.

4. And we, shall we be faithless?
  Shall hearts fail, hands hang down?
  Shall we evade the conflict,
  and cast away our crown?
  Not so: in God's deep counsels
  some better thing is stored:
  we will maintain, unflinching,
  one Church, one Faith, one Lord.

5. Thy mercy will not fail us,
  nor leave thy work undone;
  with thy right hand to help us,
  the vict'ry shall be won;
  and then by all creation,
  thy name shall be adored.
  And this shall be their anthem:
  One Church, one Faith, one Lord.

232 Lewis Hensley (1824-1905) alt.

1. Thy kingdom come, O God,
  thy rule, O Christ, begin;
  break with thine iron rod
  the tyrannies of sin.

2. Where is thy reign of peace
  and purity and love?
  When shall all hatred cease,
  as in the realms above?

Continued overleaf

3. When comes the promised time
   that war shall be no more,
   and lust, oppression, crime
   shall flee thy face before?

4. We pray thee, Lord, arise,
   and come in thy great might;
   revive our longing eyes,
   which languish for thy sight.

5. Some scorn thy sacred name,
   and wolves devour thy fold;
   by many deeds of shame
   we learn that love grows cold.

6. O'er lands both near and far
   thick darkness broodeth yet:
   arise, O morning star,
   arise, and never set.

233 Noel Richards
© 1991 Thankyou Music

1. To be in your presence,
   to sit at your feet,
   where your love surrounds me
   and makes me complete.

   This is my desire, O Lord, this is my desire,
   this is my desire, O Lord, this is my desire.

2. To rest in your presence,
   not rushing away,
   to cherish each moment,
   here I would stay.

234 Frances Jane van Alstyne
(Fanny J. Crosby) (1820-1915)

1. To God be the glory!
   great things he hath done;
   so loved he the world
   that he gave us his Son;
   who yielded his life
   an atonement for sin,
   and opened the life-gate
   that all may go in.

Praise the Lord, praise the Lord!
let the earth hear his voice;
praise the Lord, praise the Lord!
let the people rejoice:
O come to the Father,
through Jesus the Son,
and give him the glory;
great things he hath done.

2. O perfect redemption,
   the purchase of blood!
   to ev'ry believer
   the promise of God;
   the vilest offender
   who truly believes,
   that moment from Jesus
   a pardon receives.

3. Great things he hath taught us,
   great things he hath done,
   and great our rejoicing
   through Jesus the Son;
   but purer, and higher,
   and greater will be
   our wonder, our rapture,
   when Jesus we see.

235 William Chatterton Dix (1837-1898) alt.

1. To thee, O Lord, our hearts we raise
   in hymns of adoration;
   to thee bring sacrifice of praise
   with shouts of exultation:
   bright robes of gold the fields adorn,
   the hills with joy are ringing,
   the valleys stand so thick with corn
   that even they are singing.

2. And now, on this our festal day,
   thy bounteous hand confessing,
   upon thine altar, Lord, we lay
   the first-fruits of thy blessing:
   by thee our souls are truly fed
   with gifts of grace supernal;
   thou who dost give us earthly bread,
   give us the bread eternal.

3. We bear the burden of the day,
   and often toil seems dreary;
   but labour ends with sunset ray,
   and rest comes for the weary:
   may we, the angel-reaping o'er,
   stand at the last accepted,
   Christ's golden sheaves for evermore
   to garners bright elected.

4. O blessèd is that land of God,
   where saints abide for ever;
   where golden fields spread far and broad,
   where flows the crystal river:
   the strains of all its holy throng
   with ours today are blending;
   thrice blessèd is that harvest-song
   which never hath an ending.

4. 'Tis the name that whoso preacheth
   speaks like music to the ear;
   who in prayer this name beseecheth
   sweetest comfort findeth near;
   who its perfect wisdom reacheth
   heav'nly joy possesseth here.

5. Jesus is the name exalted
   over ev'ry other name;
   in this name, whene'er assaulted,
   we can put our foes to shame:
   strength to them who else had halted,
   eyes to blind, and feet to lame.

6. Therefore we in love adoring
   this most blessèd name revere,
   holy Jesus, thee imploring
   so to write it in us here,
   that hereafter, heav'nward soaring,
   we may sing with angels there.

236
'Gloriosi Salvatoris' (15th century)
trans. John Mason Neale (1818-1866) alt.

1. To the name of our salvation
   laud and honour let us pay,
   which for many a generation
   hid in God's foreknowledge lay,
   but with holy exultation
   we may sing aloud today.

2. Jesus is the name we treasure,
   name beyond what words can tell;
   name of gladness, name of pleasure,
   ear and heart delighting well;
   name of sweetness passing measure,
   saving us from sin and hell.

3. 'Tis the name for adoration,
   name for songs of victory;
   name for holy meditation
   in the vale of misery;
   name for joyful veneration
   by the citizens on high.

237
'Puer nobis nascitur'
15th century trans. Percy Dearmer, alt.
© Oxford University Press

1. Unto us a boy is born!
   King of all creation;
   came he to a world forlorn,
   the Lord of ev'ry nation,
   the Lord of ev'ry nation.

2. Cradled in a stall was he,
   watched by cows and asses;
   but the very beasts could see
   that he the world surpasses,
   that he the world surpasses.

3. Then the fearful Herod cried,
   'Pow'r is mine in Jewry!'
   So the blameless children died
   the victims of his fury,
   the victims of his fury.

Continued overleaf

4. Now may Mary's Son, who came
   long ago to love us,
   lead us all with hearts aflame
   unto the joys above us,
   unto the joys above us.

5. Omega and Alpha he!
   Let the organ thunder,
   while the choir with peals of glee
   shall rend the air asunder,
   shall rend the air asunder.

Traditional South African
v.1 trans. Anders Nyberg vs. 2 & 3 trans. Andrew Maries
© v.1 1990 Wild Goose Publications
vs 2 & 3 Sovereign Music UK

238

1. We are marching in the light of God. *(x4)*

   We are marching,
   Oo-ooh! We are marching in the light
   of God. *(Repeat)*

2. We are living in the love of God . . .

3. We are moving in the pow'r of God . . .

239

Edward Joseph Burns (b. 1938)
© The Revd. Edward J. Burns

1. We have a gospel to proclaim,
   good news for all throughout the earth;
   the gospel of a Saviour's name:
   we sing his glory, tell his worth.

2. Tell of his birth at Bethlehem,
   not in a royal house or hall,
   but in a stable dark and dim,
   the Word made flesh, a light for all.

3. Tell of his death at Calvary,
   hated by those he came to save;
   in lonely suff'ring on the cross:
   for all he loved, his life he gave.

4. Tell of that glorious Easter morn,
   empty the tomb, for he was free;
   he broke the pow'r of death and hell
   that we might share his victory.

5. Tell of his reign at God's right hand,
   by all creation glorified.
   He sends his Spirit on his Church
   to live for him, the Lamb who died.

6. Now we rejoice to name him King:
   Jesus is Lord of all the earth.
   This gospel-message we proclaim:
   we sing his glory, tell his worth.

240

William Bullock (1798-1874) and
Henry Williams Baker (1821-1877)

1. We love the place, O God,
   wherein thine honour dwells;
   the joy of thine abode
   all earthly joy excels.

2. It is the house of prayer,
   wherein thy servants meet;
   and thou, O Lord, art there
   thy chosen flock to greet.

3. We love the sacred font;
   for there the holy Dove
   to pour is ever wont
   his blessing from above.

4. We love thine altar, Lord;
   O what on earth so dear?
   For there, in faith adored,
   we find thy presence near.

5. We love the word of life,
   the word that tells of peace,
   of comfort in the strife,
   and joys that never cease.

6. We love to sing below
   for mercies freely giv'n;
   but O, we long to know
   the triumph-song of heav'n.

7. Lord Jesus, give us grace
   on earth to love thee more,
   in heav'n to see thy face,
   and with thy saints adore.

241
Matthias Claudius (1740-1815)
trans. Jane Montgomery Campbell (1817-1878) alt.

1. We plough the fields and scatter
the good seed on the land,
but it is fed and watered
by God's almighty hand:
he sends the snow in winter,
the warmth to swell the grain,
the breezes and the sunshine,
and soft, refreshing rain.

All good gifts around us
are sent from heav'n above;
then thank the Lord, O thank the Lord,
for all his love.

2. He only is the maker
of all things near and far;
he paints the wayside flower,
he lights the evening star;
he fills the earth with beauty,
by him the birds are fed;
much more to us, his children,
he gives our daily bread.

3. We thank thee then, O Father,
for all things bright and good:
the seed-time and the harvest,
our life, our health, our food.
Accept the gifts we offer
for all thy love imparts,
and, what thou most desirest,
our humble, thankful hearts.

242
John Henry Hopkins (1820-1891), alt.

1. We three kings of Orient are;
bearing gifts we traverse afar;
field and fountain, moor and mountain,
following yonder star.

O star of wonder, star of night,
star with royal beauty bright,
westward leading still proceeding,
guide us to thy perfect light.

2. Born a King on Bethlehem plain,
gold I bring, to crown him again,
King for ever, ceasing never,
over us all to reign.

3. Frankincense to offer have I,
incense owns a Deity nigh,
prayer and praising, gladly raising,
worship him, God most high.

4. Myrrh is mine, its bitter perfume
breathes a life of gathering gloom;
sorrowing, sighing, bleeding, dying,
sealed in the stone-cold tomb.

5. Glorious now behold him arise,
King and God and sacrifice;
alleluia, alleluia,
earth to heav'n replies.

243
Joseph Medlicott Scriven (1819-1886)

1. What a friend we have in Jesus,
all our sins and griefs to bear!
What a privilege to carry
ev'rything to him in prayer!
O what peace we often forfeit,
O what needless pain we bear,
all because we do not carry
ev'rything to God in prayer!

2. Have we trials and temptations?
Is there trouble anywhere?
We should never be discouraged:
take it to the Lord in prayer!
Can we find a friend so faithful,
who will all our sorrows share?
Jesus knows our ev'ry weakness –
take it to the Lord in prayer!

Continued overleaf

3. Are we weak and heavy-laden,
   cumbered with a load of care?
   Jesus only is our refuge,
   take it to the Lord in prayer!
   Do thy friends despise, forsake thee?
   Take it to the Lord in prayer!
   In his arms he'll take and shield thee,
   thou wilt find a solace there.

244 Joseph Addison (1672-1719) alt.

1. When all thy mercies, O my God,
   my rising soul surveys,
   transported with the view, I'm lost
   in wonder, love and praise.

2. Unnumbered comforts to my soul
   thy tender care bestowed,
   before my infant heart conceived
   from whom those comforts flowed.

3. When in such slipp'ry paths I ran
   in childhood's careless days,
   thine arm unseen conveyed me safe,
   to walk in adult ways.

4. When worn with sickness oft hast thou
   with health renewed my face;
   and when in sins and sorrows sunk,
   revived my soul with grace.

5. Ten thousand thousand precious gifts
   my daily thanks employ,
   and not the least a cheerful heart
   which tastes those gifts with joy.

6. Through ev'ry period of my life
   thy goodness I'll pursue,
   and after death in distant worlds
   the glorious theme renew.

7. Through all eternity to thee
   a joyful song I'll raise;
   for O! eternity's too short
   to utter all thy praise.

245 Sydney Carter (b. 1915)
© 1965 Stainer & Bell Ltd.

1. When I needed a neighbour,
   were you there, were you there?
   When I needed a neighbour,
   were you there?

   And the creed and the colour
   and the name won't matter,
   were you there?

2. I was hungry and thirsty,
   were you there, were you there?
   I was hungry and thirsty,
   were you there?

3. I was cold, I was naked,
   were you there, were you there?
   I was cold, I was naked,
   were you there?

4. When I needed a shelter,
   were you there, were you there?
   When I needed a shelter,
   were you there?

5. When I needed a healer,
   were you there, were you there?
   When I needed a healer,
   were you there?

6. Wherever you travel,
   I'll be there, I'll be there,
   wherever you travel,
   I'll be there.

246 Isaac Watts (1674-1748)

1. When I survey the wondrous cross
   on which the Prince of Glory died,
   my richest gain I count but loss,
   and pour contempt on all my pride.

2. Forbid it, Lord, that I should boast,
   save in the death of Christ, my God:
   all the vain things that charm me most,
   I sacrifice them to his blood.

3. See from his head, his hands, his feet,
   sorrow and love flow mingling down:
   did e'er such love and sorrow meet,
   or thorns compose so rich a crown?

4. Were the whole realm of nature mine,
   that were an off'ring far too small;
   love so amazing, so divine,
   demands my soul, my life, my all.

247 Nahum Tate (1625-1715)

1. While shepherds watched their flocks
      by night,
   all seated on the ground,
   the angel of the Lord came down,
   and glory shone around.

2. 'Fear not,' said he, (for mighty dread
   had seized their troubled mind)
   'glad tidings of great joy I bring
   to you and all mankind.

3. To you in David's town this day
   is born of David's line
   a Saviour, who is Christ the Lord;
   and this shall be the sign:

4. The heav'nly babe you there shall find
   to human view displayed,
   all meanly wrapped in swathing bands,
   and in a manger laid.'

5. Thus spake the seraph, and forthwith
   appeared a shining throng
   of angels praising God, who thus
   addressed their joyful song:

6. 'All glory be to God on high,
   and on the earth be peace,
   goodwill henceforth from heav'n to all
   begin and never cease.'

248 Priscilla Jane Owens (1829-1899)

1. Will your anchor hold
   in the storms of life,
   when the clouds unfold
   their wings of strife?
   When the strong tides lift,
   and the cables strain,
   will your anchor drift,
   or firm remain?

   We have an anchor
   that keeps the soul
   steadfast and sure
   while the billows roll;
   fastened to the rock
   which cannot move,
   grounded firm and deep
   in the Saviour's love!

2. Will your anchor hold
   in the straits of fear,
   when the breakers roar
   and the reef is near?
   While the surges rage,
   and the wild winds blow,
   shall the angry waves
   then your bark o'erflow?

3. Will your anchor hold
   in the floods of death,
   when the waters cold
   chill your latest breath?
   On the rising tide
   you can never fail,
   while your anchor holds
   within the veil.

4. Will your eyes behold
   through the morning light,
   the city of gold
   and the harbour bright?
   Will you anchor safe
   by the heav'nly shore,
   when life's storms are past
   for evermore?

249

'Chorus novae Jerusalem' St Fulbert of Chartres (c. 1025), trans. Robert Campbell (1814-1868)

1. Ye choirs of new Jerusalem,
   your sweetest notes employ,
   the Paschal victory to hymn
   in strains of holy joy.

2. For Judah's Lion burst his chains,
   and crushed the serpent's head;
   and brought with him,
       from death's domain,
   the long-imprisoned dead.

3. From hell's devouring jaws the prey
   alone our leader bore;
   his ransomed hosts pursue their way
   where he hath gone before.

4. Triumphant in his glory now
   his sceptre ruleth all;
   earth, heav'n and hell before him bow
   and at his footstool fall.

5. While joyful thus his praise we sing,
   his mercy we implore,
   into his palace bright to bring,
   and keep us evermore.

6. All glory to the Father be,
   all glory to the Son,
   all glory, Holy Ghost, to thee,
   while endless ages run.

2. Ye blessèd souls at rest,
   who ran this earthly race,
   and now, from sin released,
   behold the Saviour's face,
   God's praises sound,
   as in his sight
   with sweet delight
   ye do abound.

3. Ye saints, who toil below,
   adore your heav'nly King,
   and onward as ye go
   some joyful anthem sing;
   take what he gives
   and praise him still,
   through good or ill,
   who ever lives.

4. My soul, bear thou thy part,
   triumph in God above:
   and with a well-tuned heart
   sing thou the songs of love;
   let all thy days
   till life shall end,
   whate'er he send,
   be filled with praise.

250

Richard Baxter (1615-1691) and John Hampden Gurney (1802-1862)

1. Ye holy angels bright,
   who wait at God's right hand,
   or through the realms of light
   fly at your Lord's command,
   assist our song,
   for else the theme
   too high doth seem
   for mortal tongue.

251

Charles Wesley (1707-1788)

1. Ye servants of God,
   your Master proclaim,
   and publish abroad
   his wonderful name;
   the name all victorious
   of Jesus extol:
   his kingdom is glorious,
   and rules over all.

2. God ruleth on high,
   almighty to save;
   and still he is nigh:
   his presence we have:
   the great congregation
   his triumph shall sing,
   ascribing salvation
   to Jesus our King.

3. Salvation to God
   who sits on the throne!
   let all cry aloud,
   and honour the Son.
   The praises of Jesus
   the angels proclaim,
   fall down on their faces,
   and worship the Lamb.

4. Then let us adore,
   and give him his right:
   all glory and pow'r,
   all wisdom and might,
   and honour and blessing,
   with angels above,
   and thanks never-ceasing,
   and infinite love.

4. O happy servants they,
   in such a posture found,
   who share their Saviour's triumph day,
   with joy and honour crowned.

5. Christ shall the banquet spread
   with his own royal hand,
   and raise each faithful servant's head
   amid th'angelic band.

253 Steffi Geiser Rubin and Stuart Dauermann
© 1975 Lillenas Publishing Co./CopyCare

You shall go out with joy
and be led forth with peace,
and the mountains and the hills
shall break forth before you.
There'll be shouts of joy
and the trees of the field shall clap,
shall clap their hands.
And the trees of the field
shall clap their hands,
and the trees of the field
shall clap their hands,
and the trees of the field
shall clap their hands,
and you'll go out with joy.

252 Philip Doddridge (1702-1751) alt.

1. Ye servants of the Lord,
   each for his coming wait,
   observant of his heav'nly word,
   and watchful at his gate.

2. Let all your lamps be bright,
   and trim the golden flame;
   gird up your loins as in his sight,
   for awesome is his name.

3. Watch! 'tis your Lord's command,
   and while we speak, he's near;
   mark the first signal of his hand,
   and ready all appear.

Indexes

Index of Authors and Sources of Text

Scriptural Index

Index of Uses

Temptation, Penitence and Forgiveness

Hope and Consolation

Healing

Suffering and Sorrow

Protection

Redemption and Salvation

The Journey of Life
(*Hymns which, being singular, do not fit under The Pilgrim Community*)

THE CHURCH
THE PEOPLE OF GOD

The Communion of Saints

The Body of Christ

The Serving Community

The Witnessing Community

The Suffering Community

The Pilgrim Community

Christian Unity

Offertory Hymn		Communion		Final Hymn	
Abba, Father, let me be	1	And now, O Father, mindful of the love	21	God's Spirit is in my heart	86
Angel-voices ever singing	24	As we are gathered	26	Go forth and tell	87
For the beauty of the earth	76	Be still, for the presence of the Lord	32	Lead us, heavenly Father, lead us	131
O worship the Lord in the		Bread of heaven, on thee we feed	39	Saviour, again to thy dear	
beauty of holiness	185	Come, Holy Ghost, our souls inspire	52	name we raise	197
		Peace, perfect peace, is the gift	186	The angel Gabriel from heaven came	211
				You shall go out with joy	253

Index of Hymns for the Common Worship Lectionary

Index of First Lines